FEATHERS ON THE BRAIN!

For David,

In the hope that he finds it amusing. pp 118-20 tell the inside story of the Centennial of Hutley Park!

[signature] 24/8/13

FEATHERS ON THE BRAIN!
a memoir

Brian Watkins

Printed in Canada

2011

The right of Brian Watkins to be identified as the author of this work has
been asserted by him in accordance with the Copyright, Designs and
Patents Act, 1988

First published 2011 by Hardwick Hill Publishing
and printed in Canada
by
Oscar's Books,
Vancouver, British Columbia

ISBN 978-0-9866421-5-9

CONTENTS

FOREWORD

On 31st January 2009, my daughter, Caroline, was married. That event changed the dynamics of family life. It seemed to me, therefore, that now might well be the time to accept the urgings of friends, particularly Clarissa Dickson-Wright, to set down some account of my rather disjointed life and career.

I do not imagine that this account will ever be published. My role was not sufficiently significant to cause anyone to consider that it should be more widely disseminated. It is written so that my beloved daughter might gain a greater insight into why her father is as he is. With her gift for logic, I have no doubt that she will, with ease, recognise what I did right and where I went wrong. This then is dedicated to Caroline.

Brian Watkins

London, March 2009

FOREWORD II

As the original Foreword suggests, it was not my intention to publish this memoir. However, there has been some pressure from my family to make it available more widely. I have, therefore, agreed to do so. I am grateful to the Foreign and Commonwealth Office for agreeing to the publication of my account of my service as a member of Her Majesty's Diplomatic Service. I am also grateful to Jane Blakelock who so patiently typed and retyped the several drafts, and to my son in law, Christopher, who typeset it.

One thing I have learned over the years is that one must not take oneself too seriously; but, it is helpful to have someone close who will, if need be, remind one and bring one down to earth if the head seems to swell too much. That role was played admirably by my darling wife. She coined and when necessary directed at me the phrase "Feathers on the brain!", a reference to the white ostrich feathers in ambassadorial headgear. Hence, the title of this short account of a fulfilling and fascinating life. I hope that those who read it will find it of some interest.

Brian Watkins

London, November 2010

CHAPTER 1

EARLY YEARS

I was born in Newport, Monmouthshire on 26th July 1933, a year of some significance. In January of that year, Adolf Hitler became Chancellor of Germany. That event was to affect, often to blight, the lives of so many millions of people. It even impacted, albeit in a modest way, on my own life.

My parents were ordinary, hard working folk. My mother had been, as was said in those days "in service" with the Borough Architect of my home town. After her marriage in 1928, that kindly man set her up in the tobacconist/newsagent/general store which bore her name and which she ran for him. My father, nine years younger than my mother, was a skilled steel worker at Lysaght's Works. That was later, in the Second World War, to exempt him from military service.

The area where we lived, although on a main road rather than a side street, was a close knit little community. Our house was typical of the terrace style houses so familiar in most British towns. A tiny front garden, usually paved over, with a long passageway through the building. The four rooms on the ground floor, usually described as the front room, middle room, kitchen and back kitchen with an outside lavatory and three bedrooms. In our case, the front room and front area had long since been converted into a double-fronted shop. The shop had advertisement

1

mirrors. One I particularly remember featured a Victorian sailor and lauded the advantages of Players Navy Cut cigarettes. Many years later I saw one in the window of an antique shop in New York priced at five hundred dollars! The corner of the back kitchen was dominated by a boiler, literally for its function was to boil clothes. We were, however, very modern in that we had a washing machine. Not one that any modern housewife would recognise. It was a large metal box standing on four metal legs. At the back was a small wringer so unlike the large, usually, unwieldy mangle so common then. For a small boy the greatest feature was the handle on the lid of the washing machine. It was remarkably like the driver's handle of the trams which still plied the streets of my home town. It was moved side to side to agitate the clothes in the machine. For me it was not a chore to manipulate it. I was a tram driver; what joy! At the rear of the houses were long, narrow gardens eventually replete with Anderson shelters complete with bunk beds. Ours was the scene of many happy hours of imaginative play.

At the town end of the block were allotments. Our house was nearer that end. In the house next to the allotments lived my friend, Alan Markey. At the other end of the block were shops including a barber's, the sub-post office and a butcher's owned by another Watkins. Although no relation, the son of the house, Desmond, is my oldest friend with whom I remain in close touch although he now lives in Marbella. Unbelievable, although it seems today, two doors from our home was an archway leading into stables where Mr Millard, a grain merchant, kept his delivery horses. Across the road stood a chemist shop owned by Mr Crowther who later qualified as a doctor. His son, Tom, although a few years younger than I, was also a friend. He later became a Circuit Judge and Recorder of Bristol. He lives near us in Monmouthshire. Opposite the allotments stood the Baptist Chapel whence I was dispatched each Sunday afternoon to Sunday School.

Much further along Corporation Road toward Lysaght's Works were two parks, Crowther Park and the much larger Coronation Park. Despite our urban environment we had access to green open spaces. Next to the Elementary School which I attended was the public Carnegie Library. The treasures it contained were to provide me with many hours of enjoyment. St Andrew's Church had a scout troop and cub pack. Although not an Anglican in those days, I was a member of the cubs and although I never reached the exalted rank of a "sixer", I was a very proud "seconder".

My father's family originated from the small villages of Llanerfyl and Llanbrynmair, in Montgomeryshire, mid-Wales. With the exception of my grandfather, all my ancestors in the male line were born and raised in Wales. Although my mother and maternal grandfather were born and raised in Wales, my maternal line hails from a small village in Gloucestershire. Although very proud of my Welsh ancestry and to call myself Welsh, I suppose that in truth, like so many of us in the UK, I am really a mongrel. My family tree as far as we can trace it in the male line appears at Appendix A.

Early childhood memories are often patchy and disjointed. Some from those very early years have stayed with me. In December 1935, five days before Christmas, my sister, Jean was born. I always felt sorry for her because her birthday so close to Christmas seemed to me to deprive her of birthday presents. Oddly, my earliest memories surround her birth. Shortly after that event, she was very ill indeed. She nearly died, not that I was aware of that at the time. I remember, however, being very upset that my beloved grandmother hurrying to visit her ignored me in the street outside our home. I also recall being most put out when I was given a half-crown and told to give it to my new baby sister.

Next to the chemist shop opposite our house was a patch of open land where in 1938 a row of very modern bow-fronted houses was built. They were very superior to ours which only had gas lighting and an outside toilet. Lighting the gas mantles was always a trial. I seemed to be rather heavy-fisted, often breaking the fragile mantles when tasked with lighting them.

The open land was the site of the 1937 Coronation Tea Party. I remember it, I suppose, because one of our neigh-bours who had celebrated too well blundered into the tea party and rather frightened us little ones. I also recall, be-ing taken by my father to the town centre to see the King and Queen on their visit to Newport. I was on my father's shoulders in the press of people gathered to pay homage to the new Sovereign. The memory is a fleeting one of a large black car, and none at all of its royal occupants.

One of the tasks which befell me as a boy in common with many others like my cousin, Horace, later a very suc-cessful architect, was to carry a billy can of tea to my father at his work. In those years before nationalisation, the steel works were still owned by the Lysaght family. The seniors of that clan, known to their employees as Master Edward and Master Desmond were in my imagination very power-ful figures. They were, in fact, rather good employers. The workers had access to a club and institute, now alas rather dilapidated.

Both the Lysaghts were High Sheriffs of the county, their Coats of Arms adorning the room which I was later to oc-cupy in the Civic Centre. I often wonder what my father and his brothers would say were they to see my Coat of Arms on the wall with those of their late employers.

There were special occasions each year to which we children looked forward. One was the annual Whitsun

March and subsequent "Treat". The march of all the local churches was a colourful one with each contingent headed by its large banner proclaiming its denominational allegiance. The march, however, was but a prelude to the treat on Whitsun Monday, then a public holiday. For that, Sunday School children gathered at a local park or beauty spot for sports and a large tea.

The other was the annual club outing to the seaside, usually Barry Island. My father like most manual workers liked his beer. He never used pubs, but was a staunch supporter of the Gwent Club and Institute, further along our road towards town. Each summer, on a Saturday, the club members' children were taken by charabanc on the outing. To me Barry Island in those days seemed a paradise with its beach replete with donkey rides and a fairground.

Another annual event I much enjoyed was the Royal Gwent Hospital carnival and fete. In those days before the National Health Service, the hospital raised money through that and in other ways. My father, through his works, was a contributor which in those days entitled him to free hospital treatment should he need it. He never did, although, I do recall that he spent some time in a sanatorium. I assume, but do not know, with TB.

When I was just less than five, my maternal grandparents celebrated their Golden Wedding. I was there, but only recall it because I was taken ill. My cousin, Roy, was deputed to take me for a walk in the fresh air along the lane which ran behind my grandparents' house, where I was sick!

The Baptist Chapel was the scene of my greatest triumph and deepest shame. There were those who thought that I had rather a good boy soprano voice and so I was asked to sing solos at the special services held to mark the Sunday School Anniversary each year. Whatever the quality of my voice, I had great difficulty in singing to piano accompaniment. On one awful occasion, I so lost track of when I was supposed to come in, that I became upset, threw down my hymn book and flounced off the platform and out of the chapel.

Save for those early recollections, our young lives were uneventful until Herr Hitler launched his attack on Poland on 1st September 1939 precipitating the Second War World. That impacted on me directly, because I was on holiday with relatives of my father in Wolverhampton. They deemed it right that I should return at once to my home in South Wales. Aged six I travelled alone by train to be met at the railway station in Newport by my father. On that beautiful, warm, sunny Sunday afternoon I walked with him along the bank of the River Usk home to 404 Corporation Road, past the Campbell Steamers Landing Stage and the bus depot.

The Campbell Steamers loomed large in my early life in those years before the war. Each summer we travelled on them across the Bristol Channel to Weston-Super-Mare for a week's holiday. On one occasion I became ill whilst in Weston. In defiance of the shipping company rules, my mother took me aboard a steamer back to Newport to our family doctor, Dr Cohen. His verdict: I had measles!

Aged five I entered Corporation Road Elementary School, where my father had gone before me. Some sixty five years later, I was to return, resplendent in court dress as High Sheriff of the county, but that is a later story.

With the war came changes. We went to school only for half of each day and seemed to spend much time in air raid shelters, although Newport suffered only minimally from German bombing compared with our neighbours in Bristol and Cardiff. I recall a stick of incendiary bombs falling, almost directly opposite my home, in Dewstow Street, where the only casualty was an unfortunate cat. A landmine which did more damage and injury fell a short distance away between the Royal Ordnance factory and the main railway line from London to South Wales. Despite the relative safety of Newport, sleep was frequently interrupted by air raids necessitating trips to the Anderson shelter in our garden. The raids also meant that eventually my parents decided to send us to live with my mother's sisters, ten miles away up the Western valley to Abercarn, a small mining village whose mine had long since closed. My sister and I were separated. She to live with Aunt Edith, married to a local Labour Party activist (later Chairman of the old Monmouthshire County Council). I to Aunt Eva, married to the local Iron and Steel Trade Union Secretary. In Abercarn I remained for two years attending first, briefly, West End School and then Gwyddon School, now a Welsh medium school. In those days no-one I knew spoke Welsh save for a few words like "Losin" (sweets) which my beloved and illiterate grandmother, my mother's mother used.

During the war, of course, we had rationing of most foodstuffs. In Abercarn my aunt's cottage stood down a short lane at right angles to the High Street. Next to the entrance to our little lane was Parfitts, the butcher's. I remember going with my aunt to buy our meat ration. In those days it was expressed in pennyworths, some of which had to be taken in corned beef. I still marvel at how my aunt and later my step-mother managed to turn out nutritious meals with such scant ingredients. Of course, what most affected us youngsters was the sweet ration. Two, sometimes, four ounces a week was not very much. Fortunately, my father did not eat sweets so we benefited from a little extra. He donated his ration to us.

Life in Abercarn followed a ritual. On Fridays, a bath in the tin bath before the fire; on Saturdays, first house at a local cinema usually in the neighbouring village of Cwmcarn or more often, the Memorial Hall in the next village of Newbridge. Sunday evenings all my aunts gathered at my grandmother's house while their husbands, save for Uncle

Jim Morrish who was married to my blind Aunt Florrie, adjourned to the club. In those days pubs did not open on Sundays in Wales and every town and village had its clubs. This small boy sat on a pouffé, all ears, as my aunts tutted over the latest scandal or news of the war. My Aunt Eva's second son was serving in Gibraltar with the Royal Air Force. My idyllic existence was to be shattered in January 1942 when my mother, who I later learned had been suffering from cancer, died. She was buried in a Gentleman Only funeral, as was common in those days, in Abercarn Cemetery. Years later she was to share her grave with my beloved Aunt Eva and her husband, Phil.

In 1943 I returned to Newport to live with my father. The following year two things happened. He remarried and I passed the Scholarship Exam, later called the eleven plus. In September 1944, I crossed the old town bridge and entered for the first time Newport High School. Three months later, the school, or most of it burnt in a disastrous fire. For the rest of my time at the school we were taught in temporary buildings called "the huts" and in St Mark's church hall across the road from the foot of the school drive. Regarded as the more prestigious of the borough's two grammar schools, it had been founded in 1896 under the Welsh Intermediate Schools Act. I was to spend the next seven years there.

At the High School we were fortunate to have very good teachers and an ethos based on that of the great schools of England. Teachers, invariably called "masters", wore gowns. The school was divided into houses which were the entities for many activities, not least, sports. Our houses were named for great literary, military and scientific figures of the past. I was in Newton house. During the first year or so, only older men and occasionally women formed the staff. The younger men were still away at war. From late 1945 they gradually returned. An early form mistress was Mrs Shott, daughter of Newport's first Labour Mayor. One who returned to teach history had served in non-commissioned rank on Arctic convoys. He left us part-way through my time at the High School to become an examiner in History for the Civil Service Commission and later was to be a distinguished First Civil Service Commissioner. I met him again in that capacity after my stint as Administrator of Tristan da Cunha. My wife now serves as a Civil Service Commissioner. Such are the coincidences of life.

Shortly before the end of the European War, Newport's Conservative MP, Sir Reginald Clary died. There was a war time convention that any parliamentary vacancy would be filled by the party which had won the seat in the 1935 General Election. The Conservative candidate was Lieutenant Commander Ronald Bell. In the election the Labour and Liberal parties did not field candidates. However, he was opposed by an Independent Labour Party candidate, Bob Edwards of the Chemical Workers' Union. For some reason, my father let our empty shop to him as a committee room. It was there that I was first bitten by things political. In the event, Commander Bell won the seat. Many years later my daughter and his grand-daughter were at school together. Alas, for Commander (later Sir Ronald) Bell he lost the seat to Labour's Peter Freeman in the July General Election. Commander Bell returned to Parliament later through another, safer Conservative seat.

In May of 1945 the Second World War came to an end in Europe and in August the war against Japan ended too. To us there seemed little difference. Rationing continued then the blackout ended and the troops gradually returned, life was as drab as in the war days. In the General Election of July 1945, the first since 1935, Winston Churchill was ousted from Downing Street and his war time deputy, the unassuming Clement Attlee, leader of the Labour Party became Prime Minister. Such momentous events did affect us and I recall the excitement of my uncles at the nationalisation of the coal industry.

Apart from the disastrous fire of late 1944 and the inevitable angst of School Certificate in 1948 and Higher School Certificate in 1950, the year which stands out is 1947. That winter was one of the worst on record. Newport had snow piled up to just below my then waist level. The Corporation buses some how managed to ply, but the walk from the centre of town over the railway bridge and up Queen's Hill to school was difficult. On one occasion I temporarily lost a shoe. Thereafter, I felt very sorry for myself. That was the year too of a great shortage of coal. Living in a house whose only heating was coal fires (downstairs only), some form of it was essential. I was despatched to dredge sea coal which was really coal dust which fell over-board from lighters plying along the river Usk and which the tide brought ashore. Miserable work it was too.

By today's standards, Newport High School was a small school of some five hundred boys rigidly separated from the girls' equivalent next door. I was not an outstanding student, indeed in the early years often languishing near the bottom of the form except in History. It was there, however, that I learned the first rudimentary things about public speaking in the Literary and Debating Society under the tutelage of "Tulli" Alan, the senior Latin master. There too I was introduced to drama by "Bugs" Price, the Biology master who produced the school plays. One year I played Princess Katherine in Henry V with my friend, Jeffery Rowthorn, now a retired Episcopal Bishop, in the role of my maid, Alice. For most of my time after that, I worked backstage as Stage Manager. That was probably a comment on my acting ability!

I was not a great sportsman; Rugby did not appeal. I was however much interested in cricket. Alas, I was a complete rabbit at that game too. My enthusiasm and my knowledge of the MCC Rule Book were such that my playing colleagues and the Master in charge of school cricket continued to take me to away games as umpire/scorer. I umpired whenever the opposing team would consent to a mere boy officiating. When they insisted on a master in the role, I scored.

Having been bitten by the political bug, I later became active in the Young Liberals; in time, Chairman of the South Wales Young Liberals Federation and, on its formation, President of The Welsh League of Young Liberals. My successor in that office was Emlyn (now Lord) Hooson. That gave me a chance to visit other parts of Wales and I was able to meet such Liberal luminaries of the time as both of David Lloyd-George's daughters, Lady Megan and Lady Olwen Carey-Evans as well as Clement Davies, then Leader of the tiny parliamentary Liberal Party.

As a young Liberal, I worked energetically for the Liberal candidate in Newport at the 1950 General Election. I also recall going to Bristol to help the Liberals in the Election at which Tony Wedgewood-Benn was elected to Parliament in the Labour interest.

As Chairman of the South Wales Young Liberal Federation, I sat on the executive of the National League of Young Liberals. That met in London. As an impoverished schoolboy it wasn't easy for me. I remember on one occasion a long-distance lorry driver friend of my father, giving me a lift to London in the cab of his lorry. Heaven knows what Health and Safety would say of that today.

For a small school, the 1944 intake to Newport High School produced some great results. Four or five went on to Oxbridge. That year also produced in time two British Ambassadors, an Episcopal Bishop, a main board Director of British Steel, the Managing Director of Shell (UK) and a fellow of an Oxford College, together with numerous professionals in medicine, law, architecture, academe and the Church. One of my chums who entered the Church, John Stacey, went on to be a distinguished Army Padre. Badly wounded in Aden, he left the Army for a parish in rural Monmouthshire. Known to many as "Mad Jack" he died not long after I had met up with him again on my return to the county on retirement. Another who also had a distinguished career as an Army Padre was John Harris. He and I met again when I retired to Chepstow where he was serving as Vicar. He was later to act as my chaplain during my year as High Sheriff.

One of the disadvantages of not coming from an affluent home was missing out on many school trips. I was not able to go abroad. Indeed, my first venture from these shores was when I left by air for Sierra Leone at the age of twenty six. I did, however, one year manage to get on a trip to the Royal Shakespeare Theatre at Stratford-on-Avon although I had not paid. I suspect the supervising master deliberately miscounted his charges.

In my final year at school, my second in the Upper Sixth, I became a prefect. Prefects were elected by the teaching staff and I joined my oldest friend, Desmond who had made it at the end of the previous summer term and a number of my other friends in the little prefects' room in the by then restored school. By rota, we prefects read the lesson at the morning school assembly. In those days, the provisions of the 1944 Education Act concerning such gatherings were rigidly observed. It meant that we stood with the Headmaster on the platform with its light oak furniture in the restored school hall. Many years later I recognised the furniture on the platform of the hall of the successor school when as High Sheriff, I addressed that school at its annual Speech Day.

The one political issue on which I have strong views is grammar schools. I believe that it was a serious mistake to abolish them. They gave children from my background an opportunity to use their academic ability and provided a means of social mobility seemingly denied to poorer children today. I acknowledge that secondary modern schools were seen as inferior. That was, however, because of inadequate funding and a lack of clear educational or vocational focus. The answer was to deal with those inadequacies, not to abolish grammar schools.

I did not go up to Oxbridge. Interested in politics but with a strong leaning towards history, I could not, in those days, read for a degree in both at the old universities. I went up instead to the London School of Economics. Later, I was to go to Oxford, in other circumstances, to Worcester College. Both my children would in time savour the delights of Oxford, my son at Wadham and my daughter at my old college, Worcester.

The London School of Economics in 1951, although Professor Laski, had retired, was still regarded as a hot bed of socialism. Certainly the Students' Union was dominated by the Labour Society. Despite that, I, at that time a staunch young Liberal, became active in Union affairs. Although my politics were against me, I was President of the University of London Liberal Federation, I served successively as a Vice-President and then Deputy President of the Students' Union. I resigned from the former office in 1952 over what I regarded as an anti-Monarchist article in the student newspaper. In those days the Union met every week in the Old Theatre in the main building. They were frequently rowdy and heated. Nevertheless, I enjoyed these occasions when, as Deputy President, I took the chair. For some six weeks at the beginning of my term as Deputy I was acting President because for family reasons the President could not attend college.

Throughout my time in London, I lived in digs. In the first year in Balham and in the following two in Streatham. My landlady there had been widowed over thirty years earlier. She mothered me and my fellow lodgers and fed us for the princely sum of three pounds a week. Not being from an affluent family, not only were my fees paid but I received a full grant of two hundred and forty pounds a year. During the vacations, like most other students, I worked, in summer as a porter at Newport railway station, at Christmas for the Post Office. The extra money was welcome.

In those days, London University held an annual rag. In one of my undergraduate years, the Commissioner of Police banned it. He was concerned that there might be trouble between students and "Teddy Boys". We were incensed. It was agreed that we would march from St Paul's Cathedral to Parliament. Thousands of students duly gathered and escorted by City of London Police marched peacefully as far as Temple Bar where a line of Metropolitan bobbies awaited us. We broke through them. A second line at St Mary Le Strand was made of sterner stuff. The officer in charge simply had a few front rank marchers taken, and the rest of us scattered. We reassembled in twos and threes in Parliament Square at 8pm. Ten minutes or so later mounted police chased us away. A few fellow undergraduates appeared at Bow Street, but most of us survived a really rather tame demonstration with our reputations intact. During our good-humoured march from St Paul's to the City boundary, I was walking with a close friend. We were throwing loo rolls. I well recall him saying to me, "Brian, you know in about fifteen years we shall be terribly respectable." How right he was! He was an adviser to Lady Thatcher and is now knighted; I, a diplomat. I am sure most others in that crowd would have similar accounts to relate.

My involvement in student politics, perhaps, inevitably meant I was a less than assiduous student, something that hit home when I failed the Applied Economics paper in my Part I finals at the end of my second year. I got a rocket from the Chief Education Officer at Newport whose generous rate payers were wholly funding my way through college. I had to re-sit the paper with my Part II finals. Thankfully I passed. In the event I managed a decent upper second and left the groves of academe in the summer of 1954, only to receive three months later the rude awakening of a call-up for National Service, then two years long.

CHAPTER 2

MILITARY SERVICE

Having, whilst at school, served in the Air Training Corps, I was able to get into the Royal Air Force. Being only just twenty one and with no real idea of what I wanted to do with my life, I sought and eventually was granted a three year short service commission in the Education branch of the RAF. Before that happened, I experienced some strange set backs.

With many others, I arrived at the Induction Centre at RAF Cardington in Bedfordshire. The large hangars which had been home to the airships, R100 and R101 had become the places where callow youths were introduced to the discipline and unfamiliar ways of the armed forces. There it was that we had medical examinations and were equipped with the pale blue serge battledress of the Royal Air Force.

At Cardington it was discerned that I had scarred ear drums, not uncommon in my generation. That resulted in the medical board, after much deliberation on whether or not to exempt me from service, in classifying me A4G4, the lowest possible medical category for a serving airman. It meant no tropical service, a surprising ban given my later career. My medical category led to delay in my officer selection and I spent time training as an Air Traffic Control Clerk at RAF Shawbury in Shropshire and working in that capacity at RAF Filton in Bristol, where Bristol Aircraft Company was testing the Britannia aircraft.

From Cardington we travelled to RAF Hednesford in Cannock Chase in Staffordshire. We were greeted by yelling demi-gods who were actually Corporal Drill Instructors. After inoculations which in my case resulted in a week in the sick bay with a vaccine fever, we began our twelve weeks training. Housed in wooden barrack blocks which had floors we regularly shined with strange implements called "bumpers", we were drilled and exercised under the direction of the demi-gods. We fired rifles and mastered assault courses. Confined to camp for the first few weeks until we were deemed airmen-like enough to be seen abroad in the Queen's uniform, we took refuge after hours in the NAAFI canteen or the camp cinema. What seemed never ending did finally end. We passed out in a parade and were posted to our trade training camps. For four weeks at RAF Shawbury I learned Morse Code and Aircraft Recognition and all the other skills to make me a competent and effective cog in the great wheel of the Air Force. Posted to RAF Filton near Bristol, I kept count of the take-offs and landings of the Bristol Britannia so that in due time, Her Majesty's Treasury could collect the fees due from the Bristol Aircraft Company.

I was not destined to do it for long. My posting to the Officer Training Unit at RAF Jurby on the Isle of Man came through and with a white disc behind the RAF badge in my cap, I set off by train and ferry to Jurby there to join other hopeful officer cadets. There again began the inevitable round of seemingly endless days of drill and manoeuvres, this time from an officer's viewpoint interspersed with lectures on Air Force Regulations, RAF Etiquette and Protocol and much else besides. We also had night exercises in which I invariably got lost or was killed. Here our evenings were spent in the cadets' mess. For one whole week we camped at Point of Ayr. I learned to appreciate the warmth imparted by rum and Coca Cola!

At last I joined my fellow cadets on the pass out parade joining the commissioned ranks of the Royal Air Force to the strains of Auld Lang Syne played by the station band. Yet again I set off, this time to RAF Spittlegate, Grantham in Lincolnshire to train as an Education Officer. From there I went to my one and only substantive posting, as Station Education Officer RAF Pucklechurch, again just outside Bristol.

One great event, I recall, occurred right at the end of my time at RAF Jurby. We of the pass out squadron were told to provide the Guard of Honour mounted for the opening of Tynwald, the island's Parliament, by His Excellency the Lieutenant Governor, Sir Ambrose Dundas Flux-Dundas, late of the Indian Civil Service. It was all very impressive. Little did I imagine that a quarter of a century later, I would find myself on the other side of a Guard of Honour when I opened the Parliament of Bermuda.

The other significant event of my time at Jurby was with my fellow cadets to witness as scorers or some such the TT races which are an annual feature of life on the Isle of Man. A very exciting day for us and a blessed relief from our square bashing and lectures which were our lot before Her Majesty would be persuaded to grant us Her Commission.

When I arrived at Pucklechurch the station hosted the headquarters of Number 62 Group of Home Command and Number 2 GRSS, a technical unit. Many of the buildings were wooden, including the officers' mess and the education centre. In the latter I taught those who wished to pass various education tests necessary for promotion and some who were interested in securing "O" Levels. I ran the library and organised cultural activities. I once lost, or someone did, a library book. That led to an enquiry. About that same time Air Chief Marshal Sir Harry Broadhurst crashed a Vulcan bomber. My offence it seemed to me, in the eyes of the RAF, was the more serious. Life was pleasant, if routine, but relieved by the station commander, Wing Commander "Tinker" Measures, a Battle of Britain pilot. He had to maintain his flying pay by piloting Tiger Moths on a regular basis. He flew from a nearby station. He frequently took me flying with him. I hated flying, but could not show that. Tinker also broadened my experience in another way. The station Adjutant seemed often to be absent on courses and I was drafted in to take his place. That exposed me both to administration and to Air Force discipline as I was involved directly, or standing beside the Commanding Officer, with defaulters.

About half way through my time at Pucklechurch, the Air Force contracted, the Group headquarters disappeared and in its place came the Joint Services School of Languages. With that came a new station commander and a number of Chinese and Russian civilian instructors.

In 1957 I made two significant decisions. The first was that politics did not offer me a future and I would seek entry to the Colonial Service. The second was to marry. In October I did so and a number of my fellow officers formed an honour guard at the wedding in Newport at the church where my wife, a qualified teacher whom I had first met through the Young Liberals, worshipped. We took a basement flat in Clifton, Bristol, but within a month the landlord wanted it back for his family. He remitted the rent we had paid which was just as well, because on returning from our brief honeymoon in London, we had only one shilling and sixpence to our names. Fortunately, the RAF provided us with a sub-standard officer's quarter. In those days proper married quarters were not available to officers under twenty five and married allowance was not payable either. My wife initially commuted daily to Newport where she taught until January 1958 when she found a post near Bristol.

In June 1958 my commission ended. I had earlier sought entry to HM Overseas Civil Service as the Colonial Service had been renamed. Unlike HM Diplomatic Service or the Home Civil Service, there was no examination. Entry was by interview. The late Sir Ralph Furze had designed the entry procedures. He and those who followed him were concerned more about personal qualities than academic prowess. I was fortunate and passed the several interviews to which I was subjected at the old Colonial Office in Great Smith Street. Having been accepted we moved to Oxford and a very nice house in Summertown which we rented. I matriculated in the Sheldonian Theatre and joined Worcester College as one "in statu pupillari".

At Oxford I became for a while involved with the Union. The President lived near us in North Oxford. He was a Sri Lankan, Lakshman Kadirgamar, later Foreign Minister and alas assassinated. He encouraged me to debate. I once, and only once, spoke from the front bench in defence of a motion. I have forgotten the subject, but have never forgotten what "Cherwell" said of my performance, "Brian Watkins had a distinct ability to make clichés sound like policy". Perhaps, I would have made a successful politician after all! During my time at Oxford too, my son, Mark Gareth, was born at the Nuffield Maternity Home adjacent to the old Radcliffe Infirmary. He was healthy.

At the end of my year at Oxford clad, like all Oxford undergraduates in subfusc, I sat a series of examinations in subjects as diverse as Islamic studies, colonial and constitutional history and anthropology. There was alas neither degree nor diploma but failure was not a viable option. During the year we had also undertaken a course in motor car maintenance at the Morris works in Cowley. In that, fortunately for one such as I, not of a mechanical bent, there was no examination.

CHAPTER 3

COLONIAL SERVICE

At the end of my Oxford year, I was posted to Sierra Leone. We were to travel by sea to Freetown and with our heavy baggage already at Tilbury, a bombshell dropped. The Colonial Office, urged by the Governor, rang to say that perhaps I should not go after all. The Governor thought that Sierra Leone, already internally self-governing, would not be likely to welcome another pensionable British officer. In those days colonial officers received only half-pay (about five hundred pounds a year) until arrival in post. After several months and an appeal by me for more money which led to my receiving full pay, the Governor relented. It seems that he had consulted his ministers who had no objection at all to my presence.

Finally, we set off, by air, in a Vicker's Viscount for a new life in West Africa. The trip was lengthy. The flight landed at Lisbon, where because we were last off the plane and the stewardess had omitted to give us a transit card, an armed guard almost arrested us. Fortunately, a Portuguese-speaking BOAC lady rescued us. The flight also landed and we stayed overnight at Las Palmas on Gran Canaria. It landed again the next day at Bathurst (now Banjul) in the Gambia where I thought I'd stepped into a Turkish bath. Finally, we arrived at Lungi Airport in Port Loko district across the river from Freetown.

We spent several days in Freetown living in the Government guest house, being briefed, obtaining necessary supplies and finding a cook. Eventually we set off in a Land Rover for Kambia, headquarters of the district of that name in the north-west of the country and a few miles from the border with Guinea, lately independent of France and somewhat impoverished. To reach Kambia we travelled over rough laterite roads and crossed rivers by ferry, a grand name for a kind of floating pontoon.

Finally, some hundred plus miles from Freetown we arrived at our new home, a mud built house with no glass in its windows, only shutters. It comprised a living room, pantry wherein lived a family of rats and a bedroom with a bath in it. It was however a real enamel bath and there was a separate, flushable lavatory and some distance from the house, a cook house, the domain of our cook. Moreover as the older hands reminded us, we had electricity which had been installed only months earlier. We were not destined to remain in Kambia long.

After a few months I was moved to the next district towards Freetown, Port Loko. Here, as Assistant District Commissioner, I worked for one, Gary Philipson, the District Commissioner who was to retire before independence. He later became a distinguished civil servant in the Scottish Office. He was replaced by a bachelor officer who had left the Gold Coast (now Ghana) on that country's independence in 1957.

Life as ADC Port Loko was a round of hearing complaints in the office and hearing a round of them on trek to chiefdom headquarters. By this time and with internal self-government led by an all Sierra Leonean cabinet under the Premier, Sir Milton Margai, every chiefdom had a Native Authority to support its paramount chief and there was an elected district council. DCs were still, however, expected to check the tax returns and continued to act as

Magistrates and Coroners and to act as local agents of the national government. As Magistrates they confined themselves to dealing with guilty pleas. A legally qualified Sierra Leonean visiting Magistrate heard the others.

By the time I arrived, new administrative officers were no longer required to pass a proficiency examination in a local language. That was, I think, in retrospect, a pity although at the time I was much relieved. We were, however, required to sit and pass examinations in law and court procedures. I did pass. That was to stand me in good stead later when I decided to qualify as a solicitor. A combination of some papers I had taken as part of my degree and the examinations in Sierra Leone exempted me from most of the Part I of the Law Society's examinations.

On one occasion I stood before the professional Magistrate in what was as much my court as his. I had not qualified to drive, but needed one night to go into town. My driver was not to be found. I drove myself and blinded by oncoming lights hit a post at the side of the road. The only damage was to my car. However, word quickly spread that the DC had had an accident. Before I could inform the police, they had heard about it. It was believed to be the rather unpopular District Commissioner. When it became clear it was the naive young ADC, the Magistrate suggested we should forget all about it. Rather prissily I said, "No, I must appear in court". It was agreed that I would plead guilty to driving without a licence and be fined five pounds. I duly stood in the open-sided court house full of lorry drivers and others. My case was called first. I stood at the front just in front of the clerk and pleaded. The police inspector gave brief details and the Magistrate in a very quiet voice said, "Fined five pounds or" and in a loud voice, "three months' imprisonment". The clerk told me later that the looks of consternation on the faces behind me clearly showed that they were thinking, "If he sends the DC to prison for three months what will he do to us."

The old court messenger service which the DC previously controlled and which had enforced the law up country had been abolished. It had been replaced by extending the authority of the Sierra Leone police force to the former protectorate. Until almost the end of British Rule, Sierra Leone was divided between the colony (Freetown and its hinterland plus Bonthe Island) and the rest of the country. The colony had English law. The protectorate and its chiefdoms operated under indirect rule with both English law and native law and custom.

Trekking into the remoter areas of the district meant packing up a Land Rover with everything one might need including a tin bath. We lodged in the chiefdom rest houses. They varied greatly in amenities, but were mostly very rudimentary. For the most part the trips were uneventful, but once I had to rescue a native Authority Clerk from the wrath of a mob which accused him of falsifying or worse, "eating" their tax money.

On one occasion I decided to visit the Sierra Leone border post on the frontier road to Guinea. That formerly French territory had recently become independent of France having voted "No" in the referendum which President De Gaulle had called on the creation of a French Union with its former colonies. As a result the French had withdrawn from the country, taking everything with them allegedly including all the office supplies. At the border I met my Guinean opposite number coming to Kambia to buy groceries. His country was very poor and there was little in the way of goods available there. He spoke no English and my French was not of a high standard. However, I invited him to come and have a drink at my little house. He did so and I found him to be a most charming man. In many ways he seemed to me to be very French.

In Kambia District was the West African Rice Research Station at Rokupr. Staffed mostly by British scientists it had played an important role in the development of different rice strains, capable in Sierra Leone and elsewhere in West Africa, of producing greater yields. That was very important to people whose staple diet was rice. Some of the senior staff at Rokupr had been extras in the film of Graeme Green's book, "The Heart of the Matter".

In each chiefdom headquarters we were recipients of gifts from the Paramount Chief. Known locally as "Dash", they usually took the form of a rather scrawny chicken and some eggs. The rules required that we made a reciprocal gift, in cash. One of the nicest places in Port Loko district was Mahera near where Lungi airport stood. The rest house stood just above the beach facing the ocean. It enabled us to swim and was always a pleasure to visit. The Paramount Chief in my day was, unusually for Northern Sierra Leone, a Christian. I never detected any problems between the Muslims and Christians in Sierra Leone in my time. In Port Loko town itself there stood an Anglican church near the Paramount Chief's house. A small team of Christian missionaries, parson and two nurses, operated there.

Although northern Sierra Leone was Muslim, the capital area and most of the south was Christian. Freetown with its Creole population of the descendants of freed slaves was especially so. It had a splendid cathedral where many in the congregation were to be seen in full morning dress complete with top hats. The Bishop, Dr M N C O Scott was later also Archbishop of West Africa, one of the primates of the Anglican Communion. Unlike the north where women were excluded from chiefly office, in the south there was a woman Paramount Chief, a statuesque beauty who was highly influential well outside her chiefdom.

As my time in Port Loko drew to a close and our leave

loomed, independence came to Sierra Leone, reluctantly, if old Sir Milton were to be believed. A British qualified doctor he was in many ways a Victorian. As a young man in Newcastle he had married a British woman with whom he had a daughter. Lady Margai, only ever visited Sierra Leone once, for Sir Milton's funeral.

As independence approached, I was put in charge of the celebrations in Port Loko district headquarters. With the help of the Public Works Department we built a pillar in the centre of town to mark the event. The independence ceremony itself followed a format laid down by Sir Milton, a gathering on the sports field with the local police detachment parading. The paramount chiefs came into the headquarter's town and processed to the field with their chiefdom staffs of office. The District Commissioner declined to attend. I substituted for him resplendent in white uniform, pith helmet and sword. The Union flag was lowered in darkness to the strains of "God Save the Queen" played on a slightly cracked gramophone record and the new Sierra Leonean flag was raised in darkness and spotlit at full staff to the strains of the new national anthem played on the same gramophone. Then came what must be one of the most ironic events in the history of the end of empire. By direction of Sir Milton was sung the hymn, "Lead Kindly Light Amid the Encircling Gloom." Perhaps, he knew something we did not.

In recent years as stories of the brutalities and bestialities of the civil war emerged from that unhappy land, I have thought often of that strange choice of hymn and of another event which happened just before independence. In the months leading up to it, Sir Milton, over the protests of his colleagues, insisted that the people must be told what was happening. He ordered that the provincial Administrative Officers should go into "the bush". Not just into chiefdom headquarters' towns but to the remotest villages and read from a prepared script what was in prospect. Like all my colleagues, I did so. In one remote village after I had finished, an old man stood up at the back and said that he had no wish to be rude to the District Commissioner, but he must tell me that before my grandfather came he, as a boy, could not walk in safety from his village to the next and that when I left the same would be true again. I poo-pooed his idea. He was, however, more prescient than I.

Very shortly after those historic events of April 1961, I returned to the UK on leave for three months. At the end of it we returned to Sierra Leone, this time by sea and to a posting as ADC (Royal Visit) Bo. Bo was the largest town in the old protectorate and the centre of Mende Land. Although Sierra Leone had a number of tribes and languages, the largest two were Mende and Temne. Port Loko and Kambia were in Temne Land. Whilst at Oxford I had journeyed a day a week to the School of Oriental and African Studies in London to learn Mende, not Temne. Apart from my six months in Bo, my whole service was in the Temne-speaking areas.

Bo seemed a thriving metropolis when compared with Kambia and Port Loko. Apart from the Provincial and District Commissioners and their expert staffs, there were other Britons engaged in commerce and even American missionaries with one of whom we became good friends.

Bo normally had only one ADC. My colleague was a Sierra Leonean but for the months leading to the Queen's visit it had a second one, me to take charge of the organisation locally of the visit. It was fun and a relief from normal administrative work. Amongst the Sierra Leoneans there was a Magistrate, Banja Tejan Sie (later Sir Banja, GCMG, third and last Governor-General). I was to meet him again in 2000 at the St Michael and St George Service in St Paul's Cathedral, just a few months before his death.

The visit by Her Majesty, in her capacity as Queen of Sierra Leone, was a great success. Like most such events it is a blur save for three things. When the royal car drew up at the stand in the stadium, the NCO charged with opening the door was on the Queen's side away from the stand. The Queen sat immobile. Standing a few feet away I could hear Prince Phillip urging, in sailors' words, the Sierra Leonean Equerry to open his door so that he could get out and stand to one side to allow Her Majesty to exit on the side of the car nearer the stand where the Governor-General and the Prime Minister waited to greet her. The second was when Sir Milton decided to leave his place beside the Queen and join the native dancers, much to everyone's amusement. The third was as embarrassing as it was memorable to me. The Queen was to address an assemblage in a big hall in Bo which was being broadcast nationwide. I was charged with putting a floor microphone in front of her. I was also told in no uncertain terms that I was thereafter to back from her presence across the stage. I accomplished my task with the microphone well, judging by the large royal smile with which I was rewarded. However, as I finally reached the wall at the side of the stage having backed from the presence without tripping or falling off, I said with relief, "Thank God that's done". Only for the man standing by the wall to say, "You fool, I'm on the air". He was the broadcast journalist reporting on the events of the day and I had butted into his commentary.

After that royal visit I was posted again, back to Port Loko, this time as District Commissioner. My assistant was a Sierra Leonean. Most of my British colleagues had retired and I was destined to be not only the last British Administrative Officer recruited to Sierra Leone, but the last British District Commissioner in-post, the last of a seventy year old line. In those early months of independence little seemed to change. True, a different flag flew outside my house and my office, but my duties remained as they had been before. Sir Morris Dorman, the last British Governor, was still in Government House, renamed Fort Thornton, as Governor-General. I still heard complaints. One morning, my interpreter, Sergeant Major Jah, told me that there was one more complainant. In walked my four-year old son who spoke Temne, dressed in his miniature native costume. He complained in Temne about his local nanny!

In Port Loko, my wife was employed as a temporary teacher at the primary school, a role she greatly enjoyed. Her earnings, paid in local currency, eked out my salary and enabled us to make occasional forays to Freetown to buy imported groceries.

Mark's Temne led to the only time his mother got worried about him. On one occasion he went missing. Neither she, nor his local nanny, could find him. My wife called me and I set out to search for him too. Eventually, I found him gaily chatting in Temne to the local women who were washing clothes in the stream not too far from our compound. All was well that ended well.

One delightful man I met was the late Sir Abubakar Tafawah-Balewah, then Prime Minister of Nigeria. Just before Sierra Leone's independence he paid an official visit to Sierra Leone. At the end of the visit he was to spend the night at the small hotel at Lungi Airport before leaving early next day for home. The airport being in my district I had to look after him. Very early on the morning of his departure I called for him and took him to the restaurant for his breakfast. He invited me to join him. When I politely cried off on the grounds of the early hour, he was utterly charming and said that he entirely understood, but he had a flight before him and would take something.

With independence came aid from elsewhere than Britain. The American Peace Corps came to Sierra Leone and chose Port Loko as one area for their projects, road building and water well drilling. To welcome them we gave a party to which came the local great and the good. The volunteers were not much younger than I was. I was then twenty nine. I found them strangely stand-offish. I was surprised. I had found them a nice house in the town, smoothed the way with chiefs and their native authority staffs and welcomed them to my home. After the party, I expressed my surprise to their Director who was staying with us. He said in response that I must remember 1776. To them I embodied the British Empire against which the United States had revolted. I let it pass. It was not very long before their views changed markedly as they came up against the difficulties of helping people who often were less appreciative of their efforts than they thought was their due. Soon, they were finding their way to my house as a refuge from the town. Their disillusion became complete when one of them who had brought with him a whole suitcase of American sweets to distribute had it stolen. They did, however, accomplish much of their task and a number of places were provided with fresh, clean water that had never had it before.

Although in my time Sierra Leone was peaceful and its people warm and friendly, there was a darker side. There existed in the Northern Province, including Port Loko, secret societies particularly the notorious Leopard Society. Its members dressed in leopard skins complete with claws and under cover of darkness attacked their unsuspecting fellow citizens especially those who, for whatever reason, were perceived to be enemies. There also remained, despite the fact that most in the north were Muslims, belief in witchcraft and witch medicine. The latter was particularly potent. It was used, seemingly, often with fatal results, to search out liars. One of the most potent was Kawaka medicine. That was used for reasons I now forget on our cook who had been accused of some offence in native law. He swore that he had not done that of which he was accused. He died.

At the time that I served in Sierra Leone there was another young British administrative officer, Harry Mitchell, who left before independence concluding that Sierra Leone would not offer him a career. He went on to work in industry in the UK. A barrister by training, he was to become a QC and I was destined to meet him much later in life when we both served as Immigration Adjudicators.

Towards the end of my second tour in Port Loko, Sir Milton Margai called a General Election. His Sierra Leone Peoples' Party was opposed by the All Peoples' Congress led by Siaka Stephens. In Port Loko district which covered a very large area with about three hundred thousand people there were seven constituencies for all of which I was the Returning Officer. It was madness. First, a register of voters had to be compiled. This meant literate Sierra Leoneans visiting every village and trying to sort out who lived in each and who was eligible to vote. Then the registers for each constituency and subsequently each polling station had to be put together. The night before the election we were hectically tearing up the register pages and stapling them together to be ready for polling next day. Surprisingly, the officers and their registers reached their stations. There were no complaints, but those were simpler days. I recall only one thing from the count. For a reason I no longer recall, one man hurled abuse at me and asked, "what the - - did I think I was doing there". I responded, rather tartly, "teaching you to ask questions like that." He said no more.

All my constituencies, save one, returned APC members. The sole SLPP winner was Mr Amadu Wurie. He was to become Minister of Education. He was convinced that I had somehow fixed the election for him. I had not, I would not have known how. Nevertheless, he insisted on giving me a

Tissot watch. I still have it and it still works. I declared it to be worth less than twenty eight pounds, the maximum allowable gift.

Wurie's daughter, a Muslim, was married to a Christian, Sam Bangura, who had been on the Colonial Service course at Oxford with me. He was later to serve as Governor of the Central Bank and very sadly was executed by the President, I suspect for telling him the country was broke. The Paramount Chief of the chiefdom in which Port Loko district headquarters stood, Ali Kali Modhu III was a charming and helpful man. He too was murdered some years later during Sierra Leone's Civil War.

As my tour drew to a close, it became clear even to an optimist like me that there was no future for me in the civil service of an independent Sierra Leone. Reluctantly, therefore, I decided I must follow my British colleagues and seek early retirement. It was granted. I received a few hundred pounds compensation for loss of office and commuted my twenty eight shillings a week pension for a few more hundred pounds lump sum. I left Sierra Leone for the last time in 1963.

I was thirty years old, married with a five-year old son, unqualified, save for my degree and unemployed. I thought of trying the civil service exam in the hope of entry to the Commonwealth Relations Service. Unfortunately, that was many months away and I needed to earn money. I tried for a job as Secretary of the Forces Education Committee at Leeds University. I actually got it, but I turned it down because they offered a lower salary than I had hoped for. I regretted that, but it was too late. In the end, I decided to train as a solicitor.

Despite the premature end of my colonial service, I do not regret it. It was, at a young age, a varied and worthwhile experience, and one which no generation after mine would have. Later, I became a diplomat. There is a great difference in the work and the ethos of colonial officials and diplomats. The former, for good or ill, were part of the life of their territory in all its aspects. They were expected to be proactive in promoting the well being and the ambitions of those for whom they were responsible. Even in the twilight of empire during which I served, the colonial officer, especially the administrative officer in the field, remained an essential part of the government of his territory. The diplomat's role is, save in exceptional circumstances, a much more passive one. It is his duty to observe and to report to his political masters in Whitehall on what others are doing and to convey to those to whom he or she is accredited the views of those political masters. I count myself fortunate that the training and experience I gained so long ago in Sierra Leone was, at least twice in my later career, to serve me well in the roles I was called upon to play.

CHAPTER 4

DEAL

I needed an income and in those days only local government provided one to Articled Clerks. I was fortunate enough to obtain a place as an Articled Clerk with the Town Clerk of Deal, then a municipal borough in Kent at five hundred pounds a year. The Town Clerk, Ian Ashworth, was later Town Clerk of the County Borough of Canterbury and later still became one of the Circuit Administrators when the Crown Courts replaced the centuries old system of Quarter Sessions and Assizes. He was a kindly man who allowed me much latitude and six months' leave to study for my solicitor's finals.

I do not think I was a very good Articled Clerk. I never mastered how to take issue in the County Court to recover the monies which the Borough Treasurer thought was owed to the Mayor, Aldermen and Burgesses of Deal.

The Town Clerk was also Clerk of the Peace responsible for selecting juries and drawing indictments at Deal's own Quarter Sessions. Those duties devolved on me. They were tasks I much enjoyed. The Recorder of Deal was a Bencher of Gray's Inn, of which my wife is now a Bencher.

Whilst I was articled a review of salaries led to mine being almost doubled. I was also offered the post of Assistant Town Clerk (unqualified) with the promise of the deputy's job when I did qualify, as the Deputy Town Clerk had moved to a bigger job elsewhere. I rejected the offer saying that if I were to undertake the deputy's duties I should have his salary and job title. As a result a new deputy was appointed and I probably lost out on a career in local government.

The man who was appointed Deputy Town Clerk had an interesting history. He had spent most of his adult life working in insurance. His son intended to become a Barrister. For whatever reason, he seemed to his father, not to be progressing well. To spur him on, his father said that he would re-train as a Barrister and would beat him to the call. He did, and thus it was that in time he became the Deputy Town Clerk of Deal with whom I shared a room. In one way, I was very glad for he clearly knew how to proceed in the County Court to recover the monies owed to the good Burgesses of Deal.

Deal was a delightful place. My wife who was a teacher was employed at the local Church of England primary school which my son also attended. We were happy and it seemed that I was destined to follow a career either as a local government solicitor or, perhaps, in private practice. In the event it was not to be. Whilst articled, the Colonial Office telephoned me and asked if I would be interested in the post of Administrator of Tristan da Cunha. I said that I would, but felt that I must complete my articles first. When I had done so some nine months later I was appointed to that remote and isolated outpost of what remained of the British Empire.

CHAPTER 5

TRISTAN DA CUNHA

So in 1966 we set sail for Cape Town and thence by the South African Antarctic research ship, the "RSA", for Tristan some fifteen hundred miles west of Cape Town. That island with its population of three hundred or so had suffered a volcanic eruption in 1961. That had destroyed the beaches from which the islanders had set out to fish for crayfish which abounded in the waters round the island and the factory which had processed their catch. The islanders had been evacuated to the UK.

An isolated, rural, patriarchal community found itself in urbanised Britain. Housed in a former armed service base near Southampton, the men could only find work labouring for the Hampshire County Council. Most of the better paid jobs were in light industry where the nimbler fingers of women and girls were better employed. In time those factors and the constant pressure of media interest and of the Medical Research Council caused discontent. Investigation by scientists eventually concluded that Tristan could be re-occupied. A referendum amongst the adult islanders produced a large majority for return. All but a handful did so. Some, however, found it difficult to re-adjust to life on the island. By 1966 a number were ready to return to Britain. I met them at Cape Town docks. As I was about to leave aboard the RSA for Tristan, they were preparing to return to the UK.

After a week at sea I arrived at what was to be my home for the next three years. A former Administrator who had become General Manager of the fishing company based in Cape Town, Peter Day, had come to the island too. He swore me in. Apart from the islanders, there was an Anglican priest, a doctor, a teacher, a public works officer and a communications officer. The wife of the latter acted as an agricultural adviser. The ex-patriate community was completed by the South African Manager of the fishing company factory.

The Administrator was assisted by an elected council and an elected head man and head woman. Nominally the Tristan Group, Tristan, Nightingale, Inaccessible and Gough was a dependency of St Helena. Gough Island was more than two hundred miles south of the main Tristan Group. It had no permanent population, but did boast a South African manned weather station. With my wife and small son we visited it once. That necessitated jumping from a rubber boat on to a rocky ledge and then negotiating a sheer cliff. Arriving was alright, we all went up in baskets by crane. Unfortunately when the time came to leave the crane had developed a fault. We had to climb down a ladder at least sixty foot in length, my son clinging to a stalwart from the ship. That is not an experience I have ever wanted to repeat.

The Governor of St Helena was constitutionally also Governor of Tristan. There was, in practice, little contact between us. My dealings were direct with London. Communication with London was by telegram and letters. The latter took months since we only had visits by the RSA twice a year and in the southern summer by the fishing company ship, the Gillian Gaddings, named after the company Chairman's daughter. For four or five months a year, no ships or mail came. Telegrams were transmitted by radio through Cape Town. They posed no problem, unless they were classified when they took ages to decipher using only book cipher and one time pads.

The arrival of the RSA was always a great event since it carried bulk supplies for the island store as well as anything else we needed. In addition to the store's regular supplies, islanders were able to make special orders, particular items for their own use. My first duty after I took office was to try to sort those out. In the Prince Philip Hall, named for the Duke of Edinburgh who had visited in 1957, I stood surrounded by piles of goods. Some had lost their labels. I tried to establish who had ordered, amongst other things, a rather large pair of lady's undergarments. It seemed a long way from the glamorous adverts for Ferrero Rocher chocolates which seem to inform the public perception of diplomats. Strictly speaking, of course, I was not a diplomat.

The islanders had some quaint forms of speech such as "you all", the triple negative was another, "don't not never". The name for the Administrator was the Hadmiral. Some of them curiously distinguished husband and wife with the forms Mr Watkins, the man and Mr Watkins, the woman.

The islanders were in general a god-fearing people, regular in their attendance at the services in the small St Mary's Anglican Church. Apart, that is, from the small Roman Catholic group headed by an elderly South African lady known to all as Grannie Aggie. She had married an islander in South Africa during the Boer War. They had returned on a visit with their child. Unfortunately during it, the husband died and with no ship visit for several years, she married again and stayed.

In those years before World War II, the islanders were, per force, largely self-sufficient. The Colonial Office was disinterested and only the provision intermittently of a priest by the Society for the Propagation of the Gospel who was appointed Magistrate, provided the link with the outside world and the Sovereign to whom they were devoted. All that changed with the Second World War. The islanders insisted that the German pocket battleship "Graf Spee" passed by the island en route to what became known as the Battle of the River Plate. Alas, the inhabitants had no means of alerting the outside world. Later, the South African Navy established a weather and radio station there with two officers, a doctor and a padre. It was the latter who realised the commercial possibilities of the crayfish. After the war, the Colonial Development Corporation helped to establish a fishing enterprise. To hold the ring between the islanders and the company, the first Administrator, Sir Hugh Elliott, was appointed in 1950.

The Administrator ran everything, although in the case of the island store in my time not very successfully. Never having been very good at figures I got the pricing wrong and lost about five thousand pounds on it in the first year. I suggested that perhaps the Administrator needed a Treasurer to help him run the store and the bank as well as the government accounts. Eventually one was appointed.

Tristan islanders were fortunate. They paid no taxes. The island's administration was financed by royalties from the fishing company and the philatelic sales of postage stamps. Capital works were paid for from British aid but unlike some dependencies, there was no need for a grant in aid of administration.

Perhaps, because there was a guilt complex in Whitehall for all the years of neglect, capital aid was always forthcoming. In my time we obtained funds for a new water supply, a new school, a new hospital and even a new administration building cum library. The latter was stocked with books of all kinds courtesy of the Ranfurly Library Service. A playground for children was paid for by the Gulbenkian

Foundation. Electricity to government quarters was supplied until 10pm by the fishing company generator. We got funds to extend it to all the houses. We even tarred the few miles of village streets and part of the road to the potato patches where the staple crop was grown. That led to the importation by islanders of some motorbikes and even one motor car. It also necessitated the writing of Road Traffic legislation which was an adaptation of the St Helena Ordinance. My own official car was a sturdy Land Rover.

When one of the ex-patriate's jobs was vacant, the Administrator had to step in and do it. I found myself for several months supervising the public works. On one occasion we were without a clergyman for some time. I had to read Matins on Sundays. If, as did happen, I upset the islanders with some decision, I found myself doing so to my wife and son, the islanders absenting themselves.

To help me in my varied duties, I was fortunate to have a young island woman who had been partly educated in the Falkland Islands. She quickly taught herself typing and became my Secretary. My other help mate was Dick Swayne. He was described as my orderly. Dick acted as a messenger for me and generally helped to keep me in touch with news and views on the island. In a braid-edged black suit, he raised and lowered the flags at the Residency, a grandly named singled storey house with a green corrugated iron roof and the royal arms over the door. It was in fact a very modest house with an L-shaped sitting/dining room, a study, two bedrooms, a kitchen and bathroom. It was kept in order by Dick's daughter, Mary. All the islanders' houses were solidly built of stone with corrugated iron roofs.

Alan, our communicator whose official title was Superintendent of Post and Telegraphs, was an enthusiastic radio ham. He suggested that a local radio station would be a welcome addition to our limited social life. I agreed. Thereafter for a few hours each evening Radio Tristan da

Cunha broadcast to the island and often was picked up further afield, once in Denmark, programmes of music, local news and views and re-broadcast the BBC world news. It adopted as its signature tune, "A Scottish Soldier". That was wholly appropriate. Tristan owes its place in the British Commonwealth to a Scottish soldier, Corporal William Glass of Kelso in Scotland. He was a member of the small garrison sent to the island in 1816 by Lord Charles Somerset, Governor of the newly-acquired Cape Colony. He believed that Tristan might be used by the French to spring Napoleon I from St Helena whence he had been exiled after his defeat at Waterloo. St Helena is some fifteen hundred miles north-east of Tristan. Lord Charles' knowledge of geography must have been a bit weak or else his assessment of French abilities overly strong. When the garrison was withdrawn in 1817 Corporal Glass stayed on, perhaps fearing that his cape-coloured wife would not be well received in Kelso.

The Tristan group was discovered in the 16th century by the Portuguese explorer, Tristão da Cunha after whom the main island is named. When the British garrison arrived in 1816, they discovered an American sailor living there. He was the sole survivor of a group of three who had been marooned or ship wrecked there some years earlier. How the others died was not clear. Tom, the survivor, was reputed amongst the garrison to have a cache of gold somewhere on the island. He died while the garrison was there. Neither they nor any subsequent inhabitant has ever uncovered the treasure, if it ever existed.

The male ancestors of today's islanders were all Caucasian and numbered only six; Glass, Swayne, Rogers, Green, Lavarello and Repetto. Those remain the only surnames. Apart from Glass the others were all either shipwrecked on the island or jumped ship there. All the female ancestors, save for William Glass's wife, were ladies from St Helena. They were brought to Tristan in the early years by a friendly ship's captain. The island is on the great circle route and thus, in the 19th century, the main shipping lanes. With its fresh water and land on which to grow vegetables, Glass had seen an opportunity to develop a business supplying passing ships. It worked well until the construction of the Suez Canal.

Life on Tristan proved largely uneventful. Social life revolved around Prince Philip Hall with its bar selling cheap beer and spirits imported from South Africa. It was also the scene of occasional dances to gramophone music. Prince Philip had donated a radiogram on his visit in 1957. More traditional island dances which owed much to Scottish and Irish jigs were performed to a fiddle and an accordion played by older islanders.

In the hall there was also a weekly film show. A company overseas sent us a regular supply which lasted several months and which we then returned upon the next available ship. Initially we only had one projector necessitating an interval while reels were changed. Eventually, however, aid money bought us a second one and we felt we had a proper cinema.

Despite its largely uneventful lifestyle, there were occasional problems. One occurred early in my term when the Public Works Officer became involved in a fight with some islanders. It caused me to have to have him removed. In the same first tour the doctor's wife became unhappy with the island's life and asked to leave. That meant negotiations with London over the terms of the doctor's contract and special arrangements with the fishing company to get her away. In my second tour, a more serious event happened when one islander attacked another with a stone. Fortunately, he was not killed, but the island was horrified.

Violence was unknown before the evacuation. The complexities of a murder trial had death resulted horrified me. I resolved that we would have to have a more formal way of ensuring the peace. With London's agreement, I recruited a respected young islander as a full-time policeman. He was sent to Hendon for training. When Sergeant Albert Glass returned from Hendon, he with two other respected young men as Special Constables kept an eye on things especially at the bar. I am happy to say we had no more violent incidents in my time. We did have some drunkenness, but I could deal with that by using my power to ban people from using the bar or buying liquor from the island store.

Because of its isolated position and to protect the island from too many outside visitors, the Administrator's permission was needed for any visit. It was usually refused unless there was a purpose useful to the island behind it. There was in my time one real tourist. I was so intrigued by his plea that I agreed that he could visit. He was a retired American educator. Whilst working he had invested in a fund on which on retirement he could draw to fund visits to all the world's unusual islands. He had succeeded in his aim save for Tristan. I let him come. He duly did travelling on the RSA. I made it clear that the length of his visit was wholly dependent on the weather. The ship could only be unloaded if the weather were kind. He might be stuck on it for days waiting for the right conditions. If it deteriorated he might be marooned ashore in our rather primitive guest house until it cleared. In any event when the ship left so must he. He spent about ten days with us.

We also had for a while a young man from VSO who helped out in the school. Like other temporary inhabitants over the years he allegedly made a small contribution to the gene pool!

One of my most pleasant tasks as Administrator was to approve the designs of new postage stamps before they were submitted to Her Majesty The Queen for final approval. Not only was it a pleasant task, it was also an important one given the role played by philatelic sales in Tristan's finances.

Towards the end of my time we had a serious break-down in relations between the company and the islanders. The company employed a few salaried staff. Most of the able-bodied men save for a few, permanently employed by the Public Works Department, worked for the company as casual fishermen. Fishing was not an everyday event. It could only happen when the weather conditions were right. Many of the women and girls also worked casually in the factory processing the catch.

A rather ill-tempered dispute arose over fishing pay. The situation became rather ugly and I feared an outbreak of vi-olence. For the one and only time in the whole of my Crown service I sent a "Flash" telegram asking for a Royal Navy ship to be sent. A frigate off South America was ordered to steam to us. Fortunately, cooler heads prevailed and I was asked to arbitrate. My arbitration was accepted and the situation calmed. By the time the Royal Navy hoved to the crew had no more difficult task than to challenge the islanders to a game of soccer. I forget who won.

The great event of each year was Queen's Day, the local celebration of the Queen's Birthday which by special dis-pensation was always held in January during the southern summer; it was always advertised to be held on a specified date, or "the first fine day thereafter". In uniform I ad-dressed the island council, there was a drinks party in the residency garden, sports and a dance in the evening. The islanders were, and are, very loyal subjects of Her Majesty and very proud of their British Citizenship.

Christmas on Tristan was much like it is elsewhere in the Christian world; a public holiday but essentially one for family. Divine Service was held in St Mary's Church. One

Christmas we were invited to take lunch in an island home.
The food was somewhat different from Christmas dinner in
England. Turkey was unknown and the pudding was made
from potatoes, but was delicious for all that.

The somewhat monotonous life on Tristan was relieved
by the occasional call from a passenger liner which would
heave to offshore. We and the islanders would go aboard,
the latter in the hope of selling souvenirs to the passen-
gers. There were too, very occasional visits by HM ships
with whose captains I exchanged calls. That meant travelling out to her aboard the Administrator's launch, "The
Elizabeth Elliott" named by me for the wife of the first Administrator. She was new, courtesy of British aid funds. I
had great fun discussing her build during my leave. Having reached the ship's side, I had to climb a rope ladder
in full uniform, my cocked hat tucked into my jacket and
with my sword entrusted to Dick Swayne who accompanied
me. On one occasion, however, we enjoyed the luxury of
paying the call using the ship's helicopter, much easier. On
another occasion before we had the launch, I travelled to
and from in an island longboat. The ship decided to fire my
fifteen-gun salute as we left. I had to stand in the middle of
the longboat at the salute as we pulled further and further
away. No easy feat.

Although I never managed to visit Nightingale or Inaccessible islands I did, with my wife, climb to the peak of
Tristan. It stands over six thousand feet above the ocean.
Coming down was, if anything, worse than going up. The
side of the mountain was covered in what seemed like red
sand. We slipped and slid our way down.

As I have noted we did visit Gough Island. Following
the visit, I decided that one of the young South African
scientists ought to be made a Justice of the Peace so that

some official presence existed there. When I told the Colonial Office of my intention, it caused much flurry. Eventually, I was told that I could not make such an appointment. The Act of Settlement provided that only British subjects could hold such offices. South Africa, then being without the Commonwealth, its citizens were not considered to be British subjects, or in more modern parlance, Commonwealth citizens. How far are the reaches of Whitehall!

Two regular features of life for the islanders were the annual trips to the other side of the island where there exist the only trees - apple trees. There were rumours of what transpired amongst the islanders on these visits - apart from picking apples. I never enquired about the details! I never made the trip. The other big expedition was to Nightingale Island where the islanders caught what they called "Molly" birds. This is a trip I much regret never having made.

When I was on leave in the UK I was asked by the Commonwealth Relations Office which had absorbed the old Colonial Office to agree to an American survey party going to the island. The US Geodetic Service had a programme of satellite triangulation and wished to operate one of their units on Tristan for a year. I agreed. In return, the ship carrying the young scientists was joined by us in Miami and we sailed back to Tristan aboard her. The young men were a much welcomed addition to the small ex-patriate community. I confess that we were bemused by and envious of their supplies and equipment which included a massive freezer. I am glad to say that they gave it to the island when they left. Their great contribution to Tristan, was to establish by their triangulation process that Tristan was several hundred nautical yards from where the charts placed it!

Eventually, my three years on Tristan ended and again I left for Britain. Once more I was unemployed. A kindly official in London telling me that we had run out of empire suggested that I apply for the Diplomatic Service. The timing was such that he completed the necessary forms for me. Alas, when I reached the UK I learned that the Civil Service Commission did not even wish to interview me. Once more I had to seek a job. I was fortunate. I was interviewed for two. One was with ICI in their personnel department. The other was as a lecturer at Manchester University in the Department of Overseas Administration. I chose the latter, thus no doubt depriving myself of a career as a captain of industry.

··· CHAPTER 6 ···

MANCHESTER UNIVERSITY

The department at Manchester was part of the University but wholly funded by the Overseas Development Administration. It had two courses, one for Civil Servants from the new Commonwealth, the other for those from Latin America. My colleagues were a mixture of real academics and people like me, ex-Colonial Service. We were a small group, six or so. We operated in a rather ramshackle but cosy old house opposite the Manchester Eye Hospital. My duties were light, some lectures on British Government, a few tutorials and some seminars. I spent much of my time acquiring by tape, a knowledge of Spanish. The department later paid for me to attend a language school in Barcelona for three months during the summer vacation. My family joined me and we lived not far from a beach in a flat belonging to the school's Director, in Castel del Fels, a village some miles from Barcelona. I travelled to and fro each week day by bus. The students of the school were from many different countries. Our common language seemed to be English and outside class I fear we practised Spanish far less than we should have done. Happily for me my family ate most evenings in the small restaurant in the village where per force I had to try my still rather rudimentary Spanish.

At Manchester life was pleasant. I had bought my first house in the suburb of Bramhall connected by train to

Manchester. My colleagues were congenial. The Senior
Common Room was friendly. On the staff in my time were
Professor Julian Farrand and his wife (now Baroness Hale
of Richmond, a Justice of the Supreme Court) whom I was
to meet again much later through my second wife. Another
with whom I became friendly was Professor Teddy Chester
CBE. He was a refugee from the nazis who had anglicised his
name. I took over direction of the Latin American course
when the previous director left.

I was not destined to hold the post long. I had seen
an advertisement for over-aged entrance to the Diplomatic
Service. Despite the blow the Civil Service Commission
had delivered a year earlier I resolved to apply again. This
time they agreed to see me amongst the six hundred odd
applicants. I duly turned up in Saville Row for two days of
tests and interviews. The FCO member of the panel was
Harold (Hooky) Walker (now Sir Harold). We were split
into groups of six. One in my group I recall was a Master
at Marlborough. Another was Charles Cullimore, a personnel manager in industry. Unusually, two from our group,
Charles and I, satisfied the criteria and duly appeared before the final board. In due course I was notified that the
Civil Service Commission proposed to appoint me, as one
of nine, to Her Majesty's Diplomatic Service. It was Teddy
Chester who approached by the positive vetters during my
clearance procedure, provided a great answer. Asked if he
thought I was a communist, he said, "No", he thought I
was probably just right of centre. Then he added, "But if
he really were a communist, that is precisely the impression
he would give me if he were to infiltrate the Foreign Office".

Whilst I was at Manchester, my son, Mark reached
eleven. In those days Cheshire still had an eleven plus.
He sat it, but did not pass it well enough to qualify for
fees to be paid for either Manchester Grammar School
or Stockport Grammar School, then Direct Grant-Aided

schools. The reason for his seeming failure was that he had omitted to go to the lavatory before the examination and had to leave early to do so, thus not completing his papers. As I said at the time, that was the most expensive penny ever spent. He passed the entrance for Manchester Grammar School, but I had to pay his fees.

CHAPTER 7

FOREIGN AND COMMONWEALTH OFFICE

I gave a term's notice to the University and in April 1971, presented myself to the personnel department of the FCO in the person of Alan (now Sir Alan) Monroe, later Ambassador to Saudi Arabia. I was thirty seven years old. My son had just started at Manchester Grammar School, my wife had a job teaching in Stockport. I moved into a flat in Notting Hill Gate sharing with the younger brother of a Manchester colleague. I commuted weekends to Bramhall.

I was assigned to Defence Department whose role was close liaison with the Ministry of Defence. The department head initially was Bobby Tesh, a delightful man, alas now dead. His assistant for all of two weeks was Alan Urwick, who when I was Consul-General at Vancouver nearly twenty years later was my High Commissioner in Ottawa. We were three desk officers, one sadly now dead. The other, Jenkin Thomas, is still a good friend. I was charged with oversight of defence in the West Indies and maintenance of The War Book. The latter chartered all the steps which would have been needed should we approach war. This was at the height of the Cold War. On that aspect of my job I was assisted by the late Dalby Wickson, a retired Senior Chief Executive Officer re-engaged as a Grade 10. Together we kept the book up-to-date and looked after the Emergency

Rooms from which emergencies, usually consular ones, were managed.

I spent two and a half years happily going back and forth to the Ministry of Defence, often on the drafting of Services Assisted Evacuation Plans; on occasion to discuss policy with (now Sir) Richard Lloyd Jones.

There was, however, one serious event in which I was involved. The colony of British Honduras on the coast of Central America was always under threat from neighbouring Guatemala. Because of that we maintained a garrison of one battalion strength. Late one afternoon, a good friend at the American Embassy brought me a US State Department telegram which suggested that Guatemala was about to back up its threats with force. When he had gone I went to see my Under-Secretary and the Head of the Geographical Department to give them the information. They sent me to the MoD to seek assistance. I did so and my colleagues there asked me to return early next morning to see the Chief of the Defence Staff, Admiral of the Fleet Sir Peter Hill-Norton. After he had heard me, he said I should go with him to the Defence Secretary, Lord Carrington.

Shortly we did so and were joined by other high-ranking officers and Civil Servants. In his kindly manner Lord Carrington asked me what Sir Alec (Douglas-Home), then Foreign Secretary, wanted him to do. I suggested a reinforcement of the garrison would help. As it happened the battalion was due to be relieved. Lord Carrington agreed, therefore, that the new battalion should go out and the old one remain thus doubling the strength. It was also agreed that HMS Ark Royal then off the eastern sea board of the United States should fly her air craft over British Honduras as a deterrent. Before the decisions were reached, however, there occurred a hilarious scene. Lord Carrington got up and saying, "Where the - is British Honduras," began to spin the globe in his office. He and his high-ranking colleagues poured over it trying to identify this far away territory. As it happened the measures taken worked. Guatemala backed down and British Honduras went back to sleep. Coincidentally, that country under its new name of Belize was to play a role in the later part of my career also.

The other issue which loomed large in those first years in the Foreign Office was the independence of the Bahamas. Those islands had facilities which we and the Americans shared. Their future was of significance after Bahamian independence. A joint team from the FCO and the Ministry of Defence led by Clive Rose for us and the late Peter England, an Under-Secretary from the MoD, paid five visits in as many months to resolve the issue. I was on the team. We became such familiar figures that we were referred to locally as the Bucket and Spade Brigade. Those visits were a welcome change from the routine of Whitehall.

Although not responsible for defence matters in the NATO area, my War Book responsibilities took me to meetings in Brussels and meant I role-played in various NATO-wide paper exercises. Usually, I played the Foreign Secretary. It was heady stuff aping my elders and betters.

The time eventually came when Personnel Operations Department determined that I should be posted overseas. After an abortive attempt to send me to deal with defence-related matters in Canberra, I was sent to New York to be Director of Policy at British Information Services.

CHAPTER 8

NEW YORK

The role in New York involved supervision of the library staff headed by a UK qualified librarian, the production of a newsletter, liaison with the financial community in Wall Street and with opinion formers at the New York Times and other news media. One very pleasant aspect of the job was the need to travel throughout the United States to make speeches and to take part in television and radio broadcasts telling the good people of the United States the good news of Britain.

Of all the things that happened in my time in America several stand out. The first was being there during the final days of President Nixon's presidency and the interest which that aroused in the British form of government. Many Americans were confused and often unable to distinguish between Nixon the politician and the Office of the Presidency, held as it was in high regard. The others were events in which I took part. The first also concerned the attitudes towards President Nixon. I had been asked to speak to the Rotary Club of Des Moines, Iowa, a very large club in traditional Republican territory. They began proceedings with, "My Country 'tis of Thee." When I started my speech, I said it was kind of them to welcome me with such a familiar tune (that of God Save the Queen) but I thought that the words had lost something in translation. That went down well and my speech was well-received. I agreed to answer questions. The first came from a man at the very back of the room who asked me to spell out what each of the countries of the UK contributed to its economy. I went briefly through England, Scotland, Wales and Northern Ireland and sat down. Whereupon he said, "What about Canada?" A bit non-plussed, I stood again and said that Canada was as sovereign and independent of the UK as was the United States except that they had decided that the charming lady who was our Head of State should also be theirs. At that point a good diplomat would have sat down. I never was and went on to say, that it showed a good deal more foresight than could be said for thirteen other ex-British colonies. It brought the house down, much to the astonishment of the Club President. It was a clear insight into how President Nixon's problems were seen even in Republican territory.

Another which was heart warming happened on St Patrick's Day during the height of the three-day week. I was a guest on a morning TV show in Portland, Maine. I was to be followed by a troop of Irish dancers. With no good news to tell and with Northern Ireland very much an issue with many in the United States, I was dreading the interview. The interviewer, however, began in a kindly tone by saying, "Well Mr Watkins the old country seems to be having a hard time right now." After that it was an easy ride and even the young Irish dancers gave me beaming smiles as I passed them on the way out.

The third occurred at the National Conference of the English Speaking Union. The guest of honour and principal speaker was our Ambassador, the late Sir Peter Ramsbottom. There was a discussion on Anglo-American relations beforehand. As it was drawing to a close and Sir Peter was preparing to speak, I intervened and made what I hoped was a rousing speech. It went down well, but delayed my Ambassador. He twitted me about it afterwards, but in a most kindly manner. Whenever, afterwards I met him, he reminded me of that occasion.

Perhaps, however, the most fascinating thing that happened to me was when I appeared on a late evening radio show. In the commercial break, the interviewer asked me where I had served before. When I mentioned Tristan da Cunha, he exploded with glee saying that as a child he had been given a globe with a treasure chest of questions beneath it. One concerned Tristan with which he had become obsessed, but he had never before met anyone who had ever been there. He was so thrilled that he cancelled his other guests and asked if I would stay and talk with him about Tristan, which I did.

One incident which happened in New York might have had embarrassing repercussions. The late Princess Margaret and the Earl of Snowdon were visiting. Her Royal Highness was due to open the new offices of The Economist in the Times-Warner high-rise block in mid-town Manhattan. Waiting to greet her was the President of Times-Warner, the late Mr Ross. He was to be presented by the Earl of Drogheda, Chairman of The Economist. I was on duty looking after the media. Lord Drogheda had gone up in the lift to check on The Economist office. Suddenly, to my horror, I saw the Princess and her party coming through the doors of the building. Poor Mr Ross looked concerned. Fortunately, I had been presented to the Princess the previous evening. As she drew abreast of where we were standing I said in a loud voice, "Your Royal Highness". She stopped. I presented Mr Ross and explained briefly to Lord Snowdon what had happened. Mr Ross took them off to the lift. I heard later that as their lift doors opened on the The Economist floor, those of the lift opposite were closing on Lord Drogheda. Someone snapped my presentation of Mr Ross to the Princess.

Another potentially embarrassing event happened during Welsh Week in New York. Because I was Welsh, I was deputed to act as liaison with the Welsh Society, the City of New York and those others involved in the event. One evening following a Gymanfa Gani (Welsh Singing Festival) I noticed that a gaggle of members of the Morriston Orpheus Choir who were performing in the city as part of the Welsh Week celebrations were gathered rather noisily around the Private Secretary to the Secretary of State for Wales, Mr John (now Lord) Morris who was also in the city. Shortly thereafter the Private Secretary, John Lloyd, approached me and said that the choir seemed to be unable to pay its hotel bill. There had been some misunderstanding with the Welsh Society as to who would be responsible. He asked if I could help. Fortunately we were able to help. The bill was sent to me which meant that there were no taxes on it and the Chairman of the Welsh Development Agency who was travelling with the Secretary of State kindly agreed to pick up the tab.

One incident which illustrated vividly how young a country America is was when I was invited to give a guest lecture at the USAF Academy at Colorado Springs. As I was driven up the long drive through the Academy grounds to the Academy building the USAF officer escorting me suggested that we stop. He wished to show me something he thought would interest me. We walked away from the roadway down through some trees. In a small clearing stood a log cabin surrounded by a low white painted fence. Inside the fence were four small grave markers. The officer told me that the cabin had belonged to the first white settler in the area and that the graves were of four of his children killed by American Indians. He went on to tell me that their sibling who survived the massacre had returned to the site after the Air Force Academy, with its jet aircraft, had been built!

Life in New York was easy, pleasant and very social. I was provided with a charming apartment at 56th Street and 1st Avenue which was a great backdrop for me. I was effectively a bachelor since my wife declined to accompany me although she did pay two visits. The drifting apart which had begun when I went to the FCO increased. In the course of my next posting it was to lead to divorce.

Unfortunately for me, my boss in New York, Ham (later Sir Hamilton) White and I did not get on well. He eventually decided that I should leave at the end of my first two year tour rather than do the usual four years. Learning of my difficulties, Peter England of the Ministry of Defence by then the Senior UK civil servant in Belfast asked if I would be interested in working for him there.

··· CHAPTER 9 ···

NORTHERN IRELAND

Thus it was in 1976 I found myself in the midst of the Troubles, living in a government-owned house in Helen's Bay, County Down and commuting to Stormont Castle. The head of the division was a Ministry of Defence civil servant I knew from my Defence Department days. When he left he was followed by a former diplomat who had retired early but returned to the Home Civil Service.

In Northern Ireland, those of us who were married but unaccompanied, as I was, were allowed to fly to Great Britain each weekend unless we were on duty. Although life was a bit inhibited in those troubled times I did not feel in any particular danger. I did, however, share an office with a Northern Ireland office official who did have a bomb placed next to his house. He was given a warning and suffered no injuries unlike the house.

My responsibilities in Northern Ireland encompassed cross-border security and the non-violent activities of the paramilitaries. Both sides were involved in money making efforts running illegal drinking dens, building work scams, black taxi companies and many other dodges. I was involved also in liaising with the military particularly in Armagh. It meant visits for meetings to heavily-fortified army bases and to police headquarters. One of my less pleasant tasks was to represent the Secretary of State at the funerals of slain Ulster Defence Regiment personnel.

Although for the most part their bereaved relatives were stoic and dignified, there were very occasional incidents when I bore the brunt of fury with the powers that be.

One significant contribution I recall making to the process in Northern Ireland was a paper on the peace movement which had been started by two Catholic sisters and another was on the primacy of the police. The latter was of some importance and led eventually to the scaling back of army operations on the streets and an increase in the size of the Royal Ulster Constabulary with its gradual predominance in security matters. The other major initiative in which I was involved was the creation of the ring of steel around Belfast city centre, and the road blocks around Aldergrove Airport. Happily both long since dismantled.

I met people on both sides of the political divide, but was not involved with Sinn Féin. Most I met were trying hard to overcome the divide, but we were a long way from doing so. Of all those I met, I think I most warmed to Gerry (later Lord) Fitt of the Social Democratic and Labour Party.

The only violent incident which I recall in detail involved the shooting up of a pub by Protestant paramilitaries. Thought to be a haunt of Catholics, in fact all the patrons that night were Protestant. I was Duty Officer, the Duty Minister was Mr Dunn, a Liverpool Labour MP and Parliamentary Under Secretary of State. He had an interesting background. His father, as a young man, had been involved in the 1916 rising in Dublin. He had fled and fetched up in Liverpool. He married and had a son who when I knew him was a Minister of the Crown! Strange are the ways of history. Following the shooting, the Minister and I met the Reverend Ian Paisley at Stormont. When the Minister said, "Ian, how come those men shot up your people", Dr Paisley seemed lost for words, perhaps for the only time ever.

I was also Duty Officer the night the SAS inadvertently strayed across the Irish border. That caused something of a diplomatic problem. Fortunately for me, it fell mostly to my colleagues in the Republic of Ireland department of the FCO in London and our Embassy in Dublin to sort out.

Perhaps the most immediately distressing incident of the many of my time in Northern Ireland was the explosion in Dublin which killed our Ambassador, Mr Ewart Biggs and the Private Secretary to (now Sir) Brian Cubbon, Permanent Under Secretary of the Northern Ireland Office and seriously wounding him and the driver. We were all very distressed. I knew the young Private Secretary well. She was a great loss to the civil service. Sir Brian was a man with great strength of character and overcame his injuries much more quickly than any of us could have imagined.

I never experienced first hand any violence, but one night I went out with an RUC patrol through Belfast. Around midnight they dropped me off and I later learned that ten minutes afterwards they came under attack.

The Chief Constables with whom I dealt in my time in Belfast were Ken (later Sir Ken) Newman who went on to be Commissioner of the Metropolitan Police and upon his departure, an Ulsterman, Jack (later Sir John) Hermon. With the latter I dealt closely largely because of my authorship of the paper on police primacy. I liked him and his first wife, Jean. Both were very kind to someone who actually was a relatively junior official. I mourn his loss.

··· CHAPTER 10 ···

FOREIGN AND COMMONWEALTH OFFICE AGAIN

After just over two years in Belfast I returned to the Foreign and Commonwealth Office in London. I will not pretend I was not relieved to have left Northern Ireland. Again I found myself assigned to Defence Department, this time as Assistant Head of the Department responsible for the defence issues of the world outside the NATO area. My Head of Department was the late John Wilberforce, descendant of the great William Wilberforce. On retirement he was followed by the much loved David Gilmore (later Lord Gilmore of Thamesmead and Permanent Under Secretary of State). David died tragically young not long after his retirement. On his promotion from Head of Defence Department to Under Secretary (Defence) he was succeeded by John (now Sir John) Weston who was up at Worcester at the same time as I was.

In 1979, whilst I was serving in the FCO in London, the General Election of that year brought Mrs (now Baroness) Thatcher to power. I stood outside the FCO building in Downing Street (possible in those days) as she returned from the palace and recited the words of St Francis before entering No 10.

My second tour in Defence Department was again to provide me with many interesting issues. The two which stood out were the independence of Belize (the former British Honduras) and the independence of Rhodesia (now Zimbabwe). The latter came first. With the escalating Civil War in Rhodesia, there emerged a political will to try once more to solve the issue which had frustrated the Wilson government. The Conservative government under Mrs Thatcher with Lord Carrington as Foreign and Commonwealth Secretary and Richard (now Lord) Luce as Junior Minister convened a conference at Lancaster House attended by Ian Smith, Robert Mugabe, Joshua Nkomo, Bishop Muzarewa and others.

A necessary precursor to a political resolution was a scheme to end the fighting and to control the armed militias. Thus it was that I became involved. My colleagues in the responsible geographical department, Robin (now Lord) Renwick and Charles (now Lord) Powell were largely content to allow me to speak for the FCO on that issue. So with General Sir Martin Farndale and an old MOD friend, Roger (now Sir Roger) Jackling, son of another Sir Roger, a distinguished retired diplomat, I sat for many hours discussing with General Brian Walls, Commander of the Rhodesian Army, General Josiah Tongagara and the improbably named Lookout Masuku, a plan drawn up by Brigadier Adam Gurdon (father-in-law of Lord Lloyd Webber). It provided for a Commonwealth Monitoring Force drawn from the armies of the UK, Ghana and Fiji under the command of Major General Ackland, brother of Sir Anthony who later served both as PUS and Ambassador at Washington. The plan envisaged the monitoring force in gathering in the heavily-armed militias to camps via rendezvous points. Unbelievably, it was agreed and it worked with no serious incidents.

General Ackland whom I greatly admired wanted me to join him in Rhodesia as his political adviser. That, alas, was vetoed by my geographical colleagues who were to staff Lord Soames' office. They said plainly that they did not want the general to have any independent source of political or diplomatic advice. It was one of my few regrets that I was not able to be in Rhodesia at that historic time.

It was during the time of the Lancaster House conference that I was witness to an incident which illustrates quite how nice a person Lord Carrington is. He had flown to New York for forty eight hours for the General Assembly of the United Nations. On his return someone had the bright idea that he should have a meeting about Caribbean defence. The large table in his office was crowded with officials of all grades and departments. Opposite the Secretary of State sat the Permanent Under Secretary, Sir Michael Palliser. I sat two down from the PUS. The meeting got more and more strained. Lord Carrington who must have been nigh exhausted appeared to grow tetchy. Suddenly, he broke into a grin, leaned across to the PUS and said, "Michael my trip to New York doesn't seem to have done me much good does it?" It changed the whole atmosphere.

The independence of Belize also absorbed much of my time. The Minister, the late Nicholas Ridley, was proactive in trying to find a way in which to de-colonise Belize whilst ensuring its security from absorption by Guatemala. He floated a number of ideas, but finally agreed to try on the basis of a paper Roger Jackling and I drafted and which I rather irreverently described as a three-legged stool. The legs being; retaining a British military presence, training the Belize defence force and providing a written guarantee from a number of interested countries to consult in the event of hostile moves by Belize's big neighbour. On the latter, a number of independent Commonwealth Caribbean states agreed to sign. I was sent to Washington and Ottawa charged with trying to sign up the United States and Canada. Washington made plain that they saw the issue as essentially one for the Commonwealth and politely declined my overtures. Just as well. For when I spoke to the Under Secretary in the then Department of External Affairs in Ottawa, his first question to me was, "Are the Americans involved?" I was able to assure him that they were not and that the guarantee was a purely Commonwealth initiative. Canada subscribed and with the three-legged stool in place, Belize proceeded to independence under the aesthetic George Price as Prime Minister and with Her Majesty as Head of State represented by the delightful Dame Minita Gordon as Governor-General.

In a footnote to that achievement which happened only weeks before I left Defence Department to go abroad again, I should note that my colleagues said that if I could persuade the Ministry of Defence to provide an RAF aircraft to take the British party to the celebrations, I could go too. The Ministry of Defence did so, but I suspect it owed more to the fact that Prince and Princess Michael of Kent were to represent the Queen than to any importuning of mine.

On the flight to Belize, lunch was served. The Minister, Nick Ridley, and his wife Judy were bidden to join the royal couple in their apartment. The rest of us lunched together. The RAF stewardess served the wine which a bon viveur amongst us tried. He was astounded at its quality. When the Ridleys returned we asked how their lunch had gone. Nick with great candour told us that it had been good and the royals delightful but that the wine was very inferior! It was clear that by some administrative error we got the royal wine and the royals and their guests received the RAF plonk! On the return trip I was bidden to lunch with their Royal Highnesses. This time there was no slip up and so I enjoyed the royal tipple both ways.

Towards the end of my time, decisions were taken about the Naval dockyard in Gibraltar and the withdrawal of the naval vessel which did duty in the South Atlantic. The latter worried me. My Policy Desk Officer was much more sanguine. I remember a conversation with him when he was arguing that it would not cause the Argentinians to believe we were dropping our guard on the Falklands. I disagreed. I believed that they would so interpret our action. I went on to say that if they did and tried to, as they would say, recover the islands, I simply could not see any British Prime Minster still less the one then in office standing up in the House of Commons shrugging shoulders. However, my colleagues in the responsible Geographical Department agreed with my Desk Officer. I was only their mouthpiece with the Ministry of Defence and per force had to tell the Ministry of Defence that the FCO would not oppose their proposal. After I had left the department and was on Bermuda, of course, Argentina did invade the Falklands and Mrs Thatcher's response was a robust one. My desk officer phoned me on Bermuda and graciously conceded that he had been wrong and I right.

CHAPTER 11

BERMUDA

When I returned from that trip to Belize, I set out on my next posting, one which in personal terms was to prove of the greatest significance. I went as Deputy Governor of Bermuda where I was to meet the lovely lady who became my wife.

When I arrived, my predecessor Peter Lloyd, who was going to be Governor of the Cayman Islands, was still in office. I was told that my first important engagement was to be guest of honour at the regimental ball of the Bermuda Regiment. I was no longer married and concerned that a ball was one of the few events I could not attend unaccompanied. I sought Peter's advice as to whom I might invite to accompany me. He was married to a Bermudian. She knew her fellow islanders well. Every name he suggested she vetoed. Finally, on the day I was sworn in and he was to leave, he suddenly said, "You're Welsh aren't you?" When I responded affirmatively he told me that there was a young Welsh woman, Elisabeth Arfon-Jones, working at the Supreme Court and suggested I, "Try her". Some days later I was bidden to a party at the American Consul-General's house. I was dropped by the driver at the house which seemed deserted. Across the drive, however, was a small car with a young woman in it. She told me that if I was looking for the party, it was at the Consul-General's private beach. As I drew alongside she said, "I know who you

75

are" and gave me her name. Whereupon crassly and with no preliminary I said, "I know who you are", and asked if she would accompany me to the ball. To my delight she agreed. As she later said to me, why wouldn't she, it was a free meal. It was to be a very public event. After that initial meeting time passed and we had not met again and the ball loomed. Fortunately, she invited me to lunch to meet other Welshmen on the island including the Senior Magistrate, Gerald Price. He later became my daughter's godfather.

The night of the ball held in one of the island's grand hotels, Elbow Beach, passed well. The only hiccup was when the Regimental Sergeant Major who presided rose to introduce me. He was clearly used to using the rubric, "His Excellency the Governor and his charming wife" or "His Honour the Deputy Governor and his charming wife". After "Deputy Governor" there was a discernible pause whilst he sought for a formula to describe my companion. It was filled in an overloud whisper by her saying, "Bit of fluff"! We so enjoyed the evening that we remained to the end and took breakfast in the Sergeants' Mess. So began a relationship which thus far has lasted twenty eight years.

There was a period during my courtship of my wife when relations between us were strained. I found tea and sympathy at the home of the Attorney General, Saul Froomkin. He was a Canadian, his wife American. Staying with them was his sister, Adele. She was a great shoulder to cry on and was highly delighted when eventually Libby and I did marry.

One very unusual event I recall was a charity dinner, I think for the Bermuda Bird Society. I was guest of honour and asked to draw the tickets for the raffle. I did so. The first number drawn proved to be my own. As indeed was the second. They would not let me forego the prizes, so I decided to invite a lady sitting just in front of the platform to draw the third ticket. She did. It was hers! Quite extraordinary and needless to say I must have used up all my luck for I have rarely been successful in any subsequent raffles.

For several months after my arrival I lived in a hotel just above Government House. The lovely old house allocated to the Deputy Governor, "Montpelier" was in need of some tender loving care. The Ministry of Finance told me that the money which should have been spent in the past several years could now be spent on it. The PWD did an excellent job restoring and redecorating the house with its mass of lovely Bermuda cedar.

Unaccompanied, I needed a housekeeper and found one in the shape of an English lady who moved into the staff cottage. She was helped by a loveable Bermudian lady and they took care of me throughout my time on Bermuda.

By the time I arrived on the island, the Governor was very much a constitutional Head of State with only discretionary powers in the areas of foreign affairs, defence, the civil service and the police. Many of the powers relating to the latter had, in practice, been delegated to the Minister of Home Affairs. When I arrived, he was John (now Sir John) Swan, a black Bermudian businessman who, with his wife, Jackie, I had met at the Belize independence ceremonies. The Premier and Minster of Finance was a prominent white Bermudian businessman and banker, David (now Sir David) Gibbons. He and his wife were later to visit us both in Pakistan and in Swaziland and we remain good friends.

Given the limited role of the Governor, my own was similarly limited. Save for the occasional issue arising from Britain's control of foreign affairs and matters to do with the regiment or the small Royal Naval contingent on the island or relations with the Canadian and American military units there, it was mostly a case of being nice to people, substituting for the Governor as necessary, attending charity events and opening things.

Perhaps, the most fascinating person I met on Bermuda was the Canadian born Sir William Stephenson, "The Man Called Intrepid." During the Second World War, he had been Churchill's intelligence chief in the United States working with Bill Donovan, the legendary founder of the Office Of Strategic Services, a forerunner of the Central Intelligence Agency. When I knew Sir William he was an elderly widower, but still astute and in touch with many influential people worldwide. In a short visit in my time, then Vice President George Bush Snr. a former Director of the C.I.A. went to see him. Sir William encouraged me to visit him which I did frequently. We became friends. I greatly valued his kindness to me. Although virtually housebound, he nevertheless attended our Bermuda wedding. On her baptism in 1985, Caroline received from him a bracelet inscribed "from The Man Called Intrepid." A child of the eighties, she has a direct link with one of the great men of the forties.

Relations with the Governor did not always run smoothly nor did his with his ministers. The latter began just a few weeks after I arrived. The Governor told me that he needed a supplement to his locally-funded entertainment allowance and asked me to talk to the Ministry of Finance about it. When I enquired of the Aide-de-Campe who ran the household why more money was needed, his answer caused me some anxiety. In consequence, I asked him to accompany me to see the Financial Secretary. When I told the Financial Secretary what was needed, he said that since it was more than ten percent of the original vote he would need arguments for his Minister who would have to debate it in the House of Assembly. At that point I suggested he talk about it with the ADC, Major "Randy"

Butler of the Bermuda Regiment. I left them to it. So began a very unhappy episode in Bermuda history.

As it happened, there was a retired UK Treasury civil servant on the island advising the government on some financial matters. When David Saul reported to his Minister, David Gibbons suggested that that official should do a review of Government House and make recommendations. He did so, but the Governor did not approve of his suggestions. Thereafter, relations between Government House and the government deteriorated.

Eventually, David Gibbons asked me to forward a sealed letter to the Foreign and Commonwealth Office. When I asked him to what it related and he said the Governor, I refused. The regulations required letters to go through the Governor. I did, however, say that there were many ways of communicating with London. In due course a letter reached the Bermuda desk in the FCO. It went up the line but at some point was returned to the Desk Officer for return to Bermuda on precisely the grounds which had caused me to refuse to forward it. Fortunately, that officer sat on it. For very shortly afterwards the Permanent Under Secretary came to hear of it, and asked for it saying that a person like David Gibbons would not write lightly. The upshot was that an Under Secretary was sent to investigate. He concluded that quite apart from any financial matters, relations between Governor and ministers had broken down. The Governor was recalled for consultations.

The Queen was due to make a brief stopover at Bermuda en route to Jamaica. I was sent a telegram which I was asked to read without gloss to the Premier, by then John Swan. It being Cabinet Day I went to the Cabinet Office to do so rather than drag the Premier up to Government House. When I had finished reading, the Premier told me that I was to advise London that if the Governor returned, neither he nor any of his ministerial colleagues would be at the airport to meet Her Majesty. With the help of the Cabinet Secretary, much anguished weasel-wording of a telegram and a rather franker telephone call to the FCO, we got the essential message to London. The Governor did not return and in time, after I had left, was replaced by the late Viscount Dunrossill. Before the final dramatic end of a distinguished diplomat's long career much had happened in my own life.

Before the final act in his own drama, the Governor had asked for my recall. I left office the day after the Queen's visit. That though brief had been a bit stressful. The newspapers aboard the Royal Flight had been full of the political storm in Bermuda. Her Majesty cannot have been too pleased at the reportage on Her representative. Although the stopover was not an official visit, the Palace agreed we could dress it up a bit. Her Majesty inspected a guard of honour and drove in a landau to the terminal to meet dignitaries and to give an audience to the Premier. The Premier's wife was not on the island, so although I only had to present the Premier and the non-political officials, my wife of a few weeks had to remember the names and offices of everyone including the entire Cabinet and present them to the Duke of Edinburgh.

Towards the end of my brief time on Bermuda, the Governor injured his back and was hospitalised. He was due to open Parliament. In the event, for the first and only time in my life, I imitated the Sovereign and in diplomatic uniform travelled in the state landau with escort to open Parliament. The ceremonial closely mimicked that in London, albeit on a smaller scale. I accomplished my task, but there were two amusing incidents in the course of it. Before entering the Senate and directing Black Rod to summon the House of Assembly, I had to inspect a guard of honour

found by the Bermuda Regiment. With typical military ef-
ficiency they had enquired whether I would speak to anyone
and if so how many. I had told them that I would stop and
speak to three soldiers. After the Royal salute I set off with
Randy Butler and the Guard Commander to carry out the
inspection. As we walked along the front rank I stopped
twice to speak to soldiers. We turned along the rear rank
and I confess that my mind was on the rather long formula
I must use when shortly I would address Black Rod. Before
I realised it we were almost at the end of the rear rank and
I hadn't stopped. I did so suddenly. I found myself facing
the chest of a very tall black Bermudian soldier. My mind
went blank. Then I blurted out, "Are you as nervous as I
am?" Only for him to reply crisply, "No Sir".

After the opening Randy and I returned to the landau
for the trip back to Government House. Along Front Street
the crowds of locals and American tourists were quite thick
and greeted us warmly. As we turned into the quieter back
street there were many fewer people. On a corner further
down the street, however, I could see an older man waving
and cheering for all he was worth. So as we passed I threw
him what I hoped was a very smart salute. He simply yelled
back at me, "Not you, Butler". Randy Butler was not
only the Governor's ADC, he was perhaps the island's best
cricketer. In his presence, I didn't rank very high. It did
rather put matters in perspective.

In December of 1982, Libby, as all save the family know
her, went off on leave on a trip around the world en route
to the UK to spend Christmas with her parents. I followed
her progress with a gift of roses at each place she stopped
(except Moscow where Interflora did not operate). For a
while she thought that my interest was waning since the
number of roses seemed to go down as she crossed the US
and the Pacific until in Tokyo she had only had one. When
she reached India, however, to be greeted with what she

described as a shop full, she realised that the number of roses was not a reflection of the strength of my ardour, but rather the relative value of the US dollar at each of her stops. I had in fact, paid the same amount in dollars in each place.

I too took some leave for Christmas and flew to meet her in London. On Christmas night I asked her for the second time to marry me and this time she agreed. We were married by special licence at Marylebone Town Hall in the presence of my sister, Libby's parents and some relatives and friends on New Year's Eve 1982. We returned together to Bermuda and our marriage was blessed by a Welsh parson, the late Reverend Terry Abernethy, at Smith's Parish Church in a lovely ceremony on my late mother's birthday, 15th January 1983. The Governor's honorary ADCs formed an honour guard and they were joined at the insistence of the American CO by an American naval officer. We drove away in an open carriage to one of the lovely hotels Bermuda has for a champagne reception where Libby's father and the Premier made speeches.

I was forty nine years old, my bride was thirty two. Someone was unwise enough to say to my father-in-law that he wasn't losing a daughter, he was gaining a son. His only response was to quip, "Who wants a son at my age, especially one of his."

For a few weeks after my marriage I lived with my wife in her little cottage, having left office and vacated Montpelier, while she worked her notice. When that ended we left Bermuda for a honeymoon first in the US and then in Europe. I had been posted as Economic/Commercial and Aid Counsellor and Consul-General North-West Frontier Province and the Punjab at our Embassy at Islamabad, Pakistan.

PHOTOGRAPHS

Young Brian   *RAF service*

With Princess Margaret and Mr Ross in New York

As Acting Governor, Bermuda receiving a daffodil from the President of the Welsh Society on St David's Day

Our Bermuda wedding

85

In Pakistan

With Directors of the Lahore Chamber of Trade

Caroline then - with proud parents

Caroline now - with proud parents plus one!

On duty at the Consular Ball in Vancouver with my "naked" wife!

Presenting Credentials to HM The King of Swaziland, Mswati III

Presenting a prize with Sister Judith at the Technical School

Presenting one of the famous sewing machines

89

A conversation with King Mswati

Dancing with dignitaries at the King's birthday

90

"Are you a pirate mister!"

With some of the family after the Shrieval Service

91

··· CHAPTER 12 ···

PAKISTAN

When I told my wife of our posting she said, "Islamabad, when I went to school the capital of Pakistan was Karachi", to which I somewhat facetiously replied, "When I went to school, the capital of "Pakistan" was New Delhi."

Islamabad was a city specifically created to replace Karachi as capital. It was modern in concept and in architecture. For the most part the utilities worked and the staff in our house gave us excellent service. When we first arrived, Aziz, the bearer who was an immensely dignified man of stern appearance took one look at my wife and said sternly, "No babies". When our baby daughter did arrive, he was besotted with her.

My duties in Pakistan covered economic reporting, the promotion of British commercial interests and supervision of our aid programme of some fifty million pounds. As Consul-General Punjab and North West Frontier Province I also had nominal charge of the Consular and Entry Clearance staff. That section was well staffed. Just before the end of my three years in Pakistan, however, the UK introduced a visit visa regime and the size of the Immigration Section was trebled. We needed extra space to accommodate the new intake. The only available space was the coffin store. It was hurriedly converted.

The diversity of my role gave me ample opportunity to travel. We were able to go to Lahore every month so that

I could meet the business community there and to talk to the Chamber of Trade. We were also able to visit Peshawar on a regular basis and to see something of the work of Save the Children Fund in the Afghan refugee camps and of our aid projects. Those were in many areas and they enabled me to see much of Pakistan. My economic duties took me to the banks in Karachi.

Most of my dealings with the Pakistani Government were with the Ministries of Finance and Economic Affairs. In those days, when General Zia ul-Huq was President and martial law was still in force, foreign diplomats were only permitted to talk to and entertain officials of federal government departments with which they had official dealings. My travels, however, enabled me to meet many other Pakistanis and officials of all kinds at the provincial government level. My wife, on the other hand, was able to meet countless officials in all federal government departments. She had secured a local post with the American Embassy as the representative of the Library of Congress. In that capacity she had to visit Government departments to secure copies of all printed government material owed to the library under an agreement between the two countries. Her insights from her wide contacts were very useful to me.

Pakistan has many great monuments from many different periods of the history of the sub-continent; the Shalimar Gardens and fort in Lahore from Mogul days, the law courts and clubs from the days of the Raj. Perhaps the most awe-inspiring is the Bactrian Greek city at Taxila and the three thousand-year old Buddhist university overlooking it. We were able to visit it wading through, as we had to, a stream through which Alexander the Great had also passed some two thousand years before. We were fortunate to have as our guide Professor Dharni of the Quaid e Azam University in Islamabad.

During our time in Pakistan, it was visited by Sir Geoffrey Howe, then Foreign and Commonwealth Secretary. I was charged with arrangements for his trip to Lahore. He addressed the Chamber of Trade where the President ended his speech with the Welsh word for "welcome", "croeso" which I had taught him. Sir Geoffrey, a native of Wales, was delighted. The trip went well.

I had the privilege of serving two Ambassadors, the late Sir Oliver Forster and Dick Fyjis-Walker with whom and with whose wife Gabbi my wife and I remain firm friends.

I was not closely involved with political events in Pakistan, nor the momentous events next door in Afghanistan still under Soviet occupation. It was, however an exciting time to be in that part of the world. I served there through a military government with martial law to the formation of a civilian government under Mr Junejo. The chief minister of the Punjab was Mr Nawaz Sharif, later Prime Minister of Pakistan. His brother whom I got to know well ran a very successful family business. Another group of people to whom we became close was a family of very powerful women one of whom was a federal minister, Attila Anayatulla. They had a brother with whom we were also great friends who was a high official of Grindlay's Bank, later part of the ANZ Group. In that country where women were often thought of as less than first class citizens those women certainly stood out.

On one of my visits to Lahore, the chief of protocol asked if I would like to meet the late Benazir Bhutto. She had just returned from exile and received a huge welcome. I duly called on her at her house in Lahore. She had with her Farooq Leghari, later President of Pakistan and destined to dismiss Miss Bhutto as Prime Minister. Miss Bhutto began by haranguing me about the iniquities of the Zia regime and of his dastardly murder of her father, Zulfikar Ali Bhutto. When she finally ran out of steam and I was able to ask her questions, she came across as lightweight. Most of the answers were provided by Mr Leghari. I expressed my disappointment with her in a reporting telegram to London which described her in somewhat inelegant terms given that I was writing of a lady.

Some time later Miss Bhutto then staying in Islamabad, learned that an official of the British Embassy lived nearby. She invited him to visit her. Again, she launched into a long speech about the Zia regime. When finally she had finished, the officer, Barry Rundle, said "I am the Second Secretary (Estates), I just make sure that everything at the Embassy works properly".

I recall only two incidents where as Consul-General I became involved. The first concerned a British Pakistani girl who sought refuge at the Embassy from her abusive Pakistani husband. Since she had dual citizenship, there was little we could do. We did call in the police and they promised to investigate and have words with the family. The other happened in front of me. I was leaving the Inter-Continental hotel in Peshawar after lunch with the Chamber of Trade officials, when gun shots were fired. They were directed at a young British woman. A local man who had been drinking had tried to kidnap her. He forced her into his car, but then went round it to the driver's side. She escaped and ran for the hotel. He shot at her with a small Derenger type pistol. She was wounded in the wrist, but escaped. He drove off, smashing through the by then closed gates of the hotel. The young woman worked for Save the Children. Her assailant turned out to be well connected. As a result there were efforts made to keep him out of court by an offer of compensation, possible under Pakistani law. The young woman suffered no permanent harm and later married one of her colleagues.

Since part of my duty included Consular responsibility, I inevitably became involved with British citizens resident in Pakistan. In each city we had a warden whose role was to keep the Consular section of the Embassy in touch with our community. In Faiselabad, formerly Lyallpur, the warden was the Headmistress of Faiselabad Grammar School, a British lady married to a Pakistani engineer. I recall visiting her on one occasion. She had three daughters, two of whom in their late teens, were British citizens. They, I was not allowed to see, since their father was not present. I could only meet her fourteen-year old son. It pointed up neatly a difference in the two cultures. Another incident did the same. There was another British lady in Peshawar similarly married to a Pakistani. The atmosphere seemed a bit fraught when we visited. It later transpired that their daughter, a college graduate, had just been married against her and her mother's wishes to a relative of the father.

For our visits to Lahore and Peshawar we travelled between Islamabad and the two cities on The Grand Trunk Road, which looms large in Kipling's "Kim". It is a somewhat overblown name for a rather narrow strip of tarmac. Despite its narrowness, it was very busy. Lumbering carts pulled by bullocks vied for space with the gaudily painted lorries and buses which plied between Pakistan's several cities.

One evening when my wife was in England having our daughter I was due to attend a party at the home of the local Grindlay's bank manager, a Pakistani whose parents-in-law were great friends of ours. I had lent our bearer to him to help out, so I was surprised when there was a knock on the bedroom door. When I opened it there stood Aziz. He told me he had returned because the house had been raided, "the Pakistani Sahib" had been carted off to jail. I was puzzled. When I reached the manager's house I learned that the police had indeed raided the house and arrested him. It seemed that he had rather foolishly, in a legally dry country, issued his invitations for "cocktails". A woman at the bank with whom he had had a dispute had connections with the Martial Law Administrator. She had reported the party to him and he in turn had arranged for the police and a Magistrate to mount the raid. There were repercussions. The Chairman of Grindlay's contacted President Zia. As a consequence the police officer and Magistrate involved were posted. The manager, however, had, unusually, been hurriedly charged before anyone checked his connections. After a brief period in the cells, he was released on bail. Each week thereafter for well over a year he appeared in court, but no-one ever turned up to prosecute and he never came to trial. At the request of the general manager of Grindlay's, I gave the bank's liquor supplies, which had mostly escaped the attention of the police, refuge in my house until they could make other arrangements.

Another incident involving liquor concerned us directly. The local women's group wished to hold a dance. That could only take place on diplomatic premises, especially so since they wished to serve liquor. The event, with the Ambassador's agreement, duly took place in our garden. During it, my political counsellor colleague came to tell me that there had been a bomb threat against us. The Ambassador agreed to call in the police bomb squad to search. Before they arrived, the heavens opened and the liquor and most of the guests found refuge in the house, despite our having announced the threat. My wife suggested that since they had paid for the liquor, they would not leave even if it cost them an arm and leg, literally.

There was much hypocrisy about liquor in Pakistan. Frequent visitors to our house were the Federal Minister of the Interior, responsible for law and order and his wife. They never left until they had consumed the bottle of whisky I had placed on the table before them. One evening the minister complained bitterly that he could not get his favourite brand of whisky, Black Label, which incidentally he never had served by me. When I asked why that was, he said it was because Parliament was in session and the members were buying it all up. I asked him how many of his Parliamentary colleagues he thought drank and he said in response more than two thirds. When I then suggested that they could amend the Constitution let alone repeal prohibition, he said, "Oh we couldn't possibly do that".

Alcohol was also the catalyst for one of the strangest phenomena I have ever experienced. The Pakistani Ministry of Foreign Affairs had issued a note to Heads of Mission shortly before our arrival, asking them not to serve alcohol at functions attended by Pakistanis. The Australian Ambassador who was due to hold a large party to celebrate Australia Day shortly after the note was issued was concerned. He consulted the former Chief of Protocol, a retired former King Emperor's Commissioned Officer of the old Indian Army and himself a drinker. He cleverly advised the Ambassador that he should not serve alcohol, but pointed out that the note said only that. In consequence, the waiters carried trays of soft drinks. At the bottom of the garden was a screened off area where a table laden with alcoholic drinks stood without any staff. Thus was born what came to be known as the Australian Room. One always knew its exact location at any subsequent national day party, by the large queue of Pakistanis.

Perhaps the double standards were best summed up by my driver, Mohammed. He was literate in English having grown up in army bases. He was really too well qualified to be a driver. On an early visit to the Embassy house in Peshawar, we gave a party for the small British community, mostly aid workers. One of them complained to me that they had difficulty getting liquor supplies which it was legal for non-Muslims to have. After the party I gave him what was left of our small stock, mostly beer. Next morning as we were loading the Land Rover, Mohammed asked where the beer was. I told him I had given it to a British aid worker. Somewhat plaintively he said, "What about us Sahib?" When I suggested that as a good Muslim he did not drink, he said "Oh Sahib, you are very new, all the good Muslims are in Saudi Arabia".

One of the grandest events we attended in Pakistan was the marriage of the granddaughter of the late Field Marshal Ayub Khan. It took place on the sports field of the Abbottabad Army Base. Those bases called cantonments presented a stark contrast to many civilian town areas in Pakistan. They were unmistakable, with their straight streets, whitewashed kerbs and trees with white painted rings around them. Neat bungalows lined the roads. Inherited from the British Indian Army, they have the clear stamp of a military presence.

Another event which was to prove traumatic, not just in Pakistan, to which we were distant witnesses, was the assassination of Mrs Indira Gandhi. I was visiting Sialkot, near the Indian border and staying for a few days in Lahore. My wife had remained that day in Lahore. A very anxious Chief of Protocol tried desperately to get hold of me. For twenty four hours all Pakistan held its breath, fearful that Mrs Gandhi had been gunned down by Muslims. In the event it was Sikhs of her own bodyguard who had been responsible. It had been a very nasty moment. My wife later told me that she had been able to watch coverage of the events in India on both Pakistani and Indian television. That of Pakistan reported her death, Indian television only that she had been attacked. It will be recalled that the President of India was out of the country and there had been something of a hiatus until he could hurriedly return and set the constitutional moves in motion to replace the slain Prime Minister.

On one of my visits to Peshawar, I was given an insight into how our ancestors were regarded. I had been bidden to lunch in his office by the Commissioner Khyber Division. As I arrived, a tribal elder was leaving. The Commissioner affected an introduction in Pushtu which I did not speak. The elder and I shook hands and he went towards the door to leave. As he reached the door, he turned back and said something in Pushtu which seemed to be about me. There was a wry grin on the Commissioner's face so I asked what the elder had said. With a sheepish smile the Commissioner told me he had said, "That lot understood us a great deal better than you lot do". Our Victorian predecessors would have been very proud.

The most significant event of our time in Pakistan was the birth of our daughter Caroline. Her mother travelled to London for her confinement and was admitted to the old Westminster Hospital in Horseferry Road. At the end of May I had gone to Lahore for one of my regular visits. I was staying with American friends, E J Fischer and Laynne Lathram whom we were to meet again later in Washington en route to our Vancouver posting. At about twenty to three on the morning of 1st June I woke for no apparent reason. I had no premonition nor any special feelings, but I did not go back to sleep until five past three. Three hours later I was woken by E J who said that my mother-in-law was on the telephone. My daughter had been born at about ten minutes to eleven pm London time on 31st May (ten minutes to three am on 1st June Lahore time). It was a strange experience. I wasn't to see my daughter for about six weeks when I was able to go on leave on the return from leave of my colleague. I reached my parents-in-laws' home at Littleton Hall near Chester at about eleven at night.

Caroline was awake. She fitted along my forearm and I held her that way looking down at her. She gazed steadily back at me as if to say, "Oh you're responsible for this are you".

To help look after our daughter we were able to recruit a Norland nanny, Shílagh. She insisted on wearing her full Norland uniform. The Dutch Ambassadress who lived next door to us told us that the first time she had seen Shílagh thus dressed pushing a pram complete with parasol she thought she was seeing a mirage. It must indeed have seemed a very strange sight on Attaturk Avenue in Islamabad.

Throughout our time in Pakistan my wife had several times tried to travel up the Khyber Pass. She was always turned away. Diplomats were not allowed there. It was deemed too dangerous. She left Pakistan about two weeks before I did. In those two weeks I made my farewell visits to Karachi, Peshawar and Lahore. When I called on the Home Secretary of the North West Frontier Province he asked me if I had any regrets. When I said I was disappointed never to have been up the Khyber Pass, his response was immediate. He said that I as a Brit could not possibly go to another posting from Pakistan and say I have not visited the Khyber Pass. He picked up the telephone and ten minutes later with an armed escort for and aft, I was driven up the Pass to the officers' mess of what was still locally known as Queen Victoria's Corps of Guides. I stood outside it on the hillside overlooking the Afghan border about one kilometre away with an immaculately turned out Pakistani Major looking every inch like his British counterpart. With a wry smile and pointing towards Afghanistan, he said to me, "You do realise sir, that this is where your grandfathers were slaughtered by that lot".

What impressed me most on my Khyber Pass visit was that on the hills which enclose it are carved and painted the badges of the British and British Indian regiments which served there, still immaculately maintained. It was not until several months into our next tour in Vancouver that I could bring myself to confess to my wife that I had made it up the Khyber Pass.

Those farewell visits were insightful, for in each city I visited Karachi, Lahore and Peshawar there was rioting all for different reasons. So my time in Pakistan ended. Despite those riots for most of my time there, the country was peaceful. No doubt the peace owed much to Zia's martial law. However, whatever his faults, and I only met him once, he had a good side. That was best demonstrated in his clear love for his handicapped daughter whom he made no effort to hide. Indeed he took her with him to many military parades and other formal functions.

We realised what a very small world it is when we attended a farewell dinner given for us. My wife was chatting in Welsh to the British wife of a senior Pakistani official. They discovered that they had been at the same pre-school in Cardiff.

CHAPTER 13

VANCOUVER

From Pakistan we went with a short briefing period back in London via Washington and Ottawa to the lovely city of Vancouver on Canada's Pacific coast to take up my new appointment as British Consul-General, British Columbia and the Yukon.

Our trip to Vancouver was not without incident. Although visas are not needed for Canada by British citizens, we were provided with diplomatic ones. We arrived at Ottawa Airport on a cold December day in 1986. Although Canadians are the friendliest of people, some junior federal bureaucrats can be very bureaucratic indeed. When in answer to a question, I told the customs/immigration officer that we had heavy baggage following us by sea but could not say when it would arrive, she brusquely told me we would have to wait to see another officer. He was much more courteous and understanding and we were soon through and on our way to stay with old friends from FCO days Nigel Wenban-Smith, the DHC and his wife Charlotte Ryecroft who was serving as Commercial Counsellor. They had two boisterous young sons, Mungo and Jasper. Charlotte, alas, was tragically killed in a car accident a few years later when on a visit to Canada. The High Commissioner was Sir Derek Day whom I had also known as a Deputy Under Secretary in the office. He had, in fact, been Chief Clerk (Head of Personnel) at the time of my departure from Bermuda.

We spent a few very happy days in Ottawa and set off on a bitterly cold day through snow-bound streets for the airport with Nigel in his car. Alas, the airport was closed down because of the snow and we waited all day in the hope of the departure. The wait was in vain. There was no airport hotel in those days and in the evening we were directed to a motel some miles away. Fortunately we found a taxi which got us there. Unfortunately, it had no restaurant and we had a very hungry sixteen-month old girl. We were told that there was a McDonald's some distance along the main road. We set off trudging through the deep snow which blanketed everywhere with Caroline in my arms. Having reached the restaurant and eaten, we set off again retracing our steps to the motel. We slept well. Fortunately, the next day the airport was operating and we were able to complete the last leg of our journey to Vancouver which was to be our home for the next three years.

We were met at Vancouver Airport by my deputy, Jim Smyth, a Catholic Ulsterman. That fact was often to prove useful in those days when Northern Ireland was so much in the news. He greeted me with the words, "Oh thank God!" I knew we were a day late, but the situation had not been desperate. It turned out that his strange greeting had been inspired by the pipe I was carrying in my hand. He was a smoker and Vancouver had just introduced a no-smoking ban in buildings. My first action on entering the Consulate General was to order the no-smoking notices to be taken down in what I regarded as British territory. I said that we must make our customers comfortable. Anyone with a separate office could smoke if they chose to but should not if it would upset a visitor. Today, of course, I would not get away with such high-handed disregard for a local by-law.

Apart from Jim and me, the Consulate staff were all locally engaged. There was only one Commercial Officer and a number of other staff covering our other functions.

The management officer was David Munro whose wife had the improbable name of Marilyn. Although a delightful lady of whom we became very fond, she bore no physical resemblance to her famous namesake.

The Information Officer was one Dennis Emberley. He had an interesting history. He had been born German, but had grown up in England, served in the British Army and later had been commissioned in the Canadian Army following his emigration to Canada around 1950. His wife, Ursula, was also German. Much later, I was to learn more of the fascinating history of this remarkable man. He decided to retire when my term was up and I decided to recommend him for an MBE (which he got). Because of the time difference, it so happened that I was able to announce his MBE at a dinner party he attended on the night that the Honours' list appeared in London. In order to complete the forms for his award I had to research his personal file. On it I discovered an RCMP investigation form. It was longer than the file so it had been folded up. When I opened the file and folded it down I discovered that Dennis had been born Dieter. His whole name had been anglicised. In the spaces for the names and addresses of parents or place and date of death if deceased was recorded that both had perished in a concentration camp in 1942. I knew that Dennis was not Jewish, so I probed him further over a lunch. It transpired that one of his parents was Jewish, the other was not and would not divorce, so they were both burned to death by the Nazis. I asked him when his parents had brought him out of Germany to relatives to England and he said. "We passed through Amsterdam on 31st August 1939."

Vancouver was the pleasantest of posts. The city itself although rapidly developing with sky scraper office and apartment buildings going up, was still human scale. The residence bought for sixty four thousand dollars in the early 1960s was fake half timbered set on a rise in prestigious Drummond Drive out near the University of British Columbia. It looked like something out of the stockbroker belt of Surrey with its mock half timbering and was surrounded by a lovely but manageable garden ideal for a little girl. The house was elegant and comfortable, but with four bedrooms and a dining room only seating ten was not unmanageably large. We loved it. Generously, we were given allowances which covered a Welsh-speaking nanny for our daughter, a couple to look after the house and a Japanese garden company to tend the grounds. All the gardeners in Vancouver seemed to be Japanese just as all taxi drivers seemed to be (east) Indians.

In those days the Consul-General had no official car, but I was given an allowance to run my own. Lloyds Bank had expanded into Canada and taken over a local one across the road from the Consulate-General. I had transferred the Consulate account there. I had to buy a car since the office had declined to ship my rather ancient Daimler Sovereign. The Lloyds Manager gave me a one hundred percent interest only loan. His logic was that since I would pay no duties or sales taxes on an imported Jaguar I could sell it on departure probably at a profit and repay the loan. That is indeed what happened. The Manager of the local Jaguar dealership diverted a car for my use and I was, with the male half of our couple as driver, quickly mobile.

Vancouver had been the site of Expo86. That had closed a few weeks before my arrival. My predecessor, Stanley Stephenson, had been a very successful Consul-General and much involved with the British pavilion at Expo. One of the things he had done was to try to promote English wine. I bought from him rather a lot of what remained. It was, I regret to say, not very drinkable. I got rid of it over time by donating bottles as raffle prizes for charities. Later I did find some excellent English wine which was supplied to Buckingham Palace and the House of Commons. I imported and served it during my time there. I failed to get it onto the local market, good although the wine merchants proclaimed it to be, because it proved to be too expensive on the shelves. In those days the pound sterling was very strong.

With a comfortable home, a good office on the 8th floor of a pleasant office building at 1111 Melville Street in the heart of downtown Vancouver, reasonable allowances and a job which gave me ample scope, we thought ourselves well done by. Expo had given Vancouver a shot in the arm. Having been rather a back-water city compared with Toronto and Montreal, Vancouver discovered itself and thanks to Expo so did everyone else, not least other Canadians. To those from the colder often snow-bound cities it seemed with its mild climate, beaches and ski slopes something of a paradise. Social life blossomed and black tie events abounded. Still in many ways very British, the British Consul-General was much in demand. We lived a busy, sometimes rather hectic life. My wife frequently said, as we were driven in evening clothes in our Jaguar to some event or other, "Gosh and they actually pay us to be here". Just as frequently I responded, "Yes, but only the Queen can afford to get used to it."

Recognising that I could be misled by British Columbia's-seeming Britishness, I decided to recruit a small panel of three advisers. I called them the three wise men. One was wholly Canadian, one British resident there and one a Canadian of British birth and upbringing. They tried their best to keep me on the straight and narrow and were very useful for me to bounce ideas off. The British one, the late Ray Addington OBE (which he insisted meant Our Brian's Efforts) was the President of Kelly Douglas, a large supermarket chain of the Weston Group. He had been the dollar a year British Commissioner at Expo 86.

Vancouver is not, of course, the capital of British Columbia. That honour belongs to Victoria on Vancouver Island. Very early, therefore after our arrival, my wife and I had to travel there to pay our respects to the Lieutenant Governor, the Queen's representative and to the Premier. The latter was an immigrant from the Netherlands, William Van der Zalm. He headed the Social Credit Party. That was a coalition of federal Conservatives and federal Liberals. It had held office, save for a brief interlude, for many years. The opposition was drawn from the New Democratic Party, roughly akin to the British Labour Party.

Premier Van der Zalm welcomed us warmly and gave us lapel badges with the arms of British Columbia. When shortly afterwards we called on the Lieutenant Governor, the late Bob Rogers and his wife at Government House, my wife was wearing the lapel badges as earrings! This clearly perplexed Mrs Rogers who finally asked about them. Libby confessed what they were and was glad to remove them, they were a bit painful. We got to know the Rogers well. They were a charming couple and Bob was an ideal Viceroy. Their son, John, married to a Swedish lady, Lisa, we met later and became and remain close friends. They were, in fact, present at our daughter's wedding in Oxford in January 2009. Bob Rogers was followed as Lieutenant Governor by the late David Lam, an immigrant from Hong Kong. We also got to know and like him and his late wife, Dorothy. Other good friends we made were Alex and Janet Hart and Garde and Helen Gardom. Alex, alas no longer with us, and Garde were successively Agents General in London. After our time, Garde was also a distinguished Lieutenant Governor. Until we bought our apartment, the Harts kindly lent us their Vancouver apartment for our visits.

There had recently been a general election in British
Columbia but the one chamber parliament had not yet met.
However, the Chief of Protocol, Commander David Harris
late of the Canadian Navy took us to lunch with the Speaker
designate, John Reynolds. He was a larger-than-life politician of wide experience. He had served in the House of Commons in Ottawa and was to do so again later even serving
for a year as Leader of the Federal Opposition. We discovered that he and his wife, Yvonne, had a son, Christopher,
five days younger than our Caroline. Jokingly, thereafter
she was known as the older woman in Christopher's life.
We became great friends with the Reynolds and still are,
and like the Rogers they too attended our daughter's wedding. The children also were friends. I can still see them
at about four years of age dancing together at a party in
the Hotel Vancouver. That hotel was run by another good
friend, Michael Lambert with his wife Sally. Both originally
from the United Kingdom, they had spent many years in
various parts of North America in the hotel industry. Both
still live in Vancouver and both remain our good friends.

John Reynolds proved to be an excellent Mr Speaker,
respected by the Opposition although he belonged to the
Social Credit Party. Shortly after his election there was
held a "roast" in his honour at which the American Consul
General and I together with some eight Canadians including
Jean Chrétien later Prime Minister of Canada were invited
to speak. The Americans spoke first then all the Canadians.
I was the final speaker. I stood up to speak at about quarter
to midnight. Although I could not see the audience because
of the lights shining in my eyes, I could hear the diners
noisily leaving. I began by saying they had heard from
every shade of Canadian opinion, they had even heard from
Big Brother, it was now Mother's turn. It seemed to do
the trick. I was told later by the Party President that the
audience stopped leaving and sat down again.

John was, however, an ambitious politician. He came to me towards the end of my time and some six or seven months before a likely election. He told me that the Premier wished him to leave the Chair and join the Cabinet. He asked my view. I counselled him against. I told him that in my assessment, the Social Credit Party would have eight seats after the election. If he stayed in the Chair, he would get back and could thereafter pick up the pieces and lead a revitalised party. In the event he did join the Cabinet as Minister of the Environment, a truly poisoned chalice in British Columbia. After the election he came to see me again saying, "I should have listened to you, you were right". I said in response, "No, I wasn't John. I said eight seats, you got seven, you lost yours".

The other important early call I had to make was on the Mayor of Vancouver. He had taken office the day I arrived. He told me that he was very glad it was the British representative who called on him first. He was of Scottish descent, like so many there. Gordon Campbell (now Premier of British Columbia) was relatively young and likeable. He was to be a good Mayor. That office in Canada is a cross between the British one and the American one. The members of Council were then elected city-wide and were called Aldermen (which has since changed to Councillor) the Mayor likewise was elected city-wide. Like his British counterpart he chaired the Council and like his British counterpart he had a mayoral chain. He was also the social leader of the city with a truly hectic social life. However like his American counterpart he was the Chief Executive, the leader of the political life of the Council and I suppose a cross between a British Mayor and British Council leader. We became friends. He lived near us out by the University.

There was in Vancouver a thriving Welsh society. On St David's Day 1987 I was to speak at their annual dinner to propose the toast to Wales and St David. The Mayor was to attend to respond to the toast to the city. He arrived towards the end of dinner just before the loyal toast, proposed inevitably at all public events in British Columbia. He sent a message down the table to say he had another engagement later and could we change the order of toasts so he would speak before I proposed St David. That toast is the principal one at a Welsh event as you would expect. I sent a message back saying, "If that Scots man thinks he can spoil a Welsh event, he should think again." Graciously, he accepted my undiplomatic rebuke and St David took precedence over the city of Vancouver.

The other politician we got to know well and with whom we became great friends was the member of the legislative assembly (MLA) for the area where the residence stood. A very bright, young woman who spoke fluent French and Russian, she was a somewhat maverick member of the Social Credit Party strongly opposed to the leader. She was the source of much information. Whenever, I went to Victoria which I did about every six weeks, more frequently when Parliament was sitting, I made a bee line for her room. She would open up. So much so that I once said to her that she shouldn't really tell me what she did since I was a foreign diplomat. She said, "No you're not, you're the British Consul-General". I was reminded of that on my next posting when the same formula produced the same response. In the end I agreed that in return for her openness, I would be selective in my reporting of it. In due course, she became totally disillusioned with her party and as a federal conservative fought and won a federal by-election to the House of Commons in Ottawa. She rose rapidly. She is, the Right Honourable Kim Campbell, later Prime Minister of Canada, albeit rather briefly. She is a great lady. When I was no longer in Canada she even whilst Prime Minister, wrote me letters in her own hand.

A further event which underscored the relationship between British and Canadians occurred when we dog sat. The Commander of Maritime Forces Pacific headquartered at HMCS Esquimalt on Vancouver Island, Vice Admiral Bob George and his wife Lois became good friends. They were going on a brief leave. They had an Airedale called Tanya. Our daughter was hugely fond of Tanya and of her name which she was later to give to her own pet in Swaziland. When the Georges learned that we were to be in Victoria for the same period as they were away they suggested we dog sat. So we did, living in Admiralty House inside the naval base. I really cannot think of anywhere else where a technically foreign diplomat could be afforded such a privilege.

My experiences with political figures not only in Canada reinforced my view that what matters in international relations is the personal relationships diplomats build up. Diplomacy still needs people, not just electronic communications.

Early in our tour, our Filipino houseman fell into bad company and started drinking heavily. Marcos had formerly worked for Lord Iveagh. One evening when we were attending a civic dinner in West Vancouver, I was summoned from the head table to take a telephone call. It was from my Deputy reporting that Marcos had run amok and gone for his wife with a carving knife. The Royal Canadian Mounted Police who guarded the residence wanted permission to enter and act. I gave it, but later learned that my slightly built father-in-law who with my mother-in-law was visiting had actually disarmed Marcos. After the dinner a number of the other guests who had noticed me leaving and later returning told my wife how much they admired her total unconcern at the event. In fact being very short-sighted she had noticed nothing. It was myopia not sang froid.

Marcos spent the night in the cells. The local chief of the RCMP suggested we should dismiss him and send him back to Ireland. I agreed but also agreed to see him before he left because he wished to apologise. I sent my wife and daughter, her parents and the nanny into the city for lunch while Marcos came to the residence to apologise. I learned later from my wife that the nanny had said repeatedly over lunch, "I'm not used to this, such goings on". Finally, my exasperated mother-in-law said to her, "Oh do be quiet, do you think any of us is used to drunken butlers attacking their wives with kitchen knives!"

British Columbia and the Yukon is a very large area. We travelled it extensively, visiting places as far-flung as Prince George, Prince Rupert, Smithers, Fort St John, William's Lake, as well as Kamloops and the towns of the Okanagan Valley, which is geographically a desert, and those in the Fraser Valley much nearer to Vancouver. We also visited the many towns on Vancouver Island. We enjoyed our visits to Whitehorse the capital of the Yukon, although once in winter when the temperature was minus thirty seven degrees celsius, it felt less than welcoming. The small administration in the Yukon headed by the federally appointed Commissioner, Ken McKinnon in my day, and the Premier whose mother lived in my home county always made us very welcome. On one occasion we were taken to pan for gold dust. Our hosts generously donated what they had garnered to add to our own so that we had enough to fill a small glass locket for our young daughter.

We even visited Haida Gwaii, Queen Charlotte Islands. It was there that the local President of the First Nation showed me his Haida Gwaii passport on which he had travelled, rather than on a Canadian one. He told me that he intended to visit the UK only for me to say "not on that passport you won't!"

On two occasions we visited Dawson City, the old mining capital from gold rush days, many miles north of Whitehorse the modern capital. Dawson City still had dirt streets
and board sidewalks, but a number of elegant buildings including the opera house and the old Commissioner's residence which had been restored. Our first visit was to attend
the annual Commissioner's Ball held in the restored opera
house. It was one of the most elegant functions I have ever
attended. In black tie I was seriously underdressed. Almost all the men were in white tie and tails and the women
in gorgeous evening gowns, many in the style of the 1880s.
The ball was held at the height of summer, so that when
we left the ball at two am it was still broad daylight. We
repaired to what was then Canada's only legal casino, Dia-
mond Tooth Gertie's. I won nothing.

On that occasion we had flown in an old Dakota aircraft
hired by the Commissioner. The plane had an ample supply
of champagne. It also had what seemed like oil streaming
from its engines. I have never seen my wife consume so
much champagne and remain stone cold sober.

Our second visit was to accompany the High Commis-
sioner, Sir Alan Urwick and his wife on an official visit.
On that occasion we flew from Whitehorse to Dawson in a
small six-seater plane. I got the impression that dear Marta
(Lady Urwick) was not very enthusiastic about the flight.
They were both, however, very enthusiastic about Dawson.

Although remote from London and even from Ottawa,
we did not want for official visitors. In October 1987 the
Commonwealth Heads of Government Meeting (CHGM)
was held there. That brought Her Majesty the Queen,
Prime Minister, Mrs Margaret Thatcher, the Secretary of
State, Sir Geoffrey Howe, the Permanent Under-Secretary,
our High Commissioner and countless other officials.
Amongst the royal household were Ken (now Sir Ken)

Scot whom I had known in the United States and Robin
(now Lord Janvrin) who had served with me in Defence
Department and who when we had visited India, where he
was then posted, on a trip from Pakistan had bought our
railway tickets for us. I was not, of course, involved with
the Queen's visit to British Columbia which followed the
CHGM. She was there as Queen of Canada. I was involved
with the British delegation to the meeting. I was able to
attend the formal opening and to meet with colleagues
from London. The great issue at the meeting was sanctions
on South Africa. Mrs Thatcher's view differed totally
from that of most of her Commonwealth colleagues. The
meetings were somewhat acrimonious. However, she had
local support. An enterprising Canadian had a plane flown
over the city trailing a banner saying, "Hang in there
Maggie". Some years later, when travelling out to have
dinner with a friend at Aldergrove, the car in which I
was travelling was being driven by a friend of my host. I
discovered from him the story behind the banner. For the
driver was none other than the enterprising author of it.
Coincidences do happen!

The Queen's visit to British Columbia was highly
successful. The provincial government gave a state banquet. I was told by protocol that the government wished
my wife and me to attend. I discovered that my other
Commonwealth colleagues including the Australian and
New Zealand career Consuls General whose Queen she also
was were not being invited. I said that I did not think
it right that the British representative alone should be
invited. Much as I appreciated the honour, I would not
be able to accept unless they too were invited. In the
event, they and the career Indian Consul General and the
Honorary Fijian Consul were also bidden.

For the latter it was a sad evening. The first Fijian
coup happened about that time. The Honorary Consul,

Raj Pillai and an Indian Fijian, was in tears. Both the Queen's Private Secretary Sir William Heseltine and his deputy, Ken Scott, went out of their way to speak kindly to him.

The next day the Queen unveiled the newly augmented coat of arms of British Columbia in the Law Courts. It caused some amusement. Her Majesty when she pulled the curtain cord clearly expected them to draw apart. They didn't, they dropped and she visibly jumped startled by their unexpected movement.

Amongst other visitors were Richard (now Lord) Luce, then Arts Minister. I had known him a little when he served as a minister in the FCO. He and his wife Rose were delightful guests. They were to visit us again after he left politics in our next post and the four of us were to become friends. There was, however, one event on the programme we had arranged on which he was not keen and tried to resist. We visited Victoria and I wished him to tour the Royal British Columbia Museum. I suspected he had had his fill of museums, but I insisted. Graciously, he gave way and I left him to make the visit with the Director. When he rejoined me, he told me that it had been a great experience, I had been right to insist he visit it and he believed that British museums could learn a lot from it. I was relieved, but I knew what he meant. Our own daughter absolutely adored what I still believe is one of the finest museums in the world.

Another very gracious visitor was the late Earl of Derby and his wife. His ancestor as Lord Stanley had been Governor-General of Canada, after whom Vancouver's magnificent Stanley Park was named. Its centenary fell in our time in Vancouver. The city Parks' Board decided to invite the Earl and Countess to participate in the celebrations. Alas, the Board had no money for their accommodation, flights or car. The latter problem was solved by the free loan of a Rolls Royce by the local dealership, the flights by British Airways and the accommodation by us. They asked for separate bedrooms which did not present a problem, although I had to tell them they would have to share a bathroom. I got rather more worried when the Earl in reply accepted our offer, but said that they would be accompanied by his valet and her lady's maid. We had limited staff accommodation. Our nanny lived over the garage and our Filipino couple in the basement apartment. We had no room for their servants. Happily it was vacation time and the UBC offered to put them up in student rooms on the campus not far from us.

The Derbys enjoyed their visit. They gave us a view of aristocratic life we thought no longer existed. I doubt they had often lodged in a house in a street. Lord Derby did vouchsafe, however, that they had friends who didn't have servants. Each evening after returning from whatever function we had been at, the Derbys enjoyed a nightcap. Lady Derby initially insisted she must wash the glasses. She had great difficulty in operating the taps. In exasperation, my wife finally told her to stay out of the kitchen.

It was during this visit that Caroline was responsible for perhaps the most embarrassing incident of my career. She was three years old. Lady Derby occupied the front bedroom usually used by Caroline's grandparents on their visits. One evening Caroline did something she had never done with her grandparents. Having had a bath in our bathroom across the landing, before her nanny could catch her, she charged stark naked across it, pushed open the Derbys' door and soaking wet jumped onto the bed much to the surprise of Lady Derby. We were not quite sure how to rescue that situation. We need not have worried. Lady Derby said that she would dine out on the story of how in Vancouver she had had a nude stranger in her bed!

We were due to go on leave at the end of the Derbys'
visit, but the timing of their flight and ours was such that
they stood on the residence's doorstep waving us off.

During our leave the Derbys kindly asked to lunch at
Knowsley Hall. Since our cottage where we were staying
was in North Wales it was not a long journey. They had
urged us to bring our daughter, but we declined that offer.
The thought of a three-year old running around a stately
home with its objects d'art filled us with horror.

Another visitor was the late Alan Clarke then a Minister
at the Board of Trade. He was less easy than other visitors,
but did not stay with us. He had expressed an interest in
visiting a company involved with modern technology and
its application. We, therefore, arranged for him to visit one
in Richmond near the airport as his last engagement. The
Managing Director himself operated the apparatus and explained everything to the minister. When he had finished,
Mr Clarke said, thank you, asked not even one simple question although there were clear applications of interest to
the UK, and left. At the airport he irritably asked who had
been responsible for that visit. My deputy owned up, but
I intervened to take responsibility for what I believed was
an excellent project and entirely in line with the minister's
request.

At the time of the visit, the Canadians were considering
acquiring some ships for use in the Arctic North. There
were opportunities for British suppliers although the ships
would be Canadian built. I arranged a stag dinner party
and seated the minister at the end of the table with the
two most important figures involved with the contract on
either side of him. After the main course he and I changed
places. To my astonishment the two guests told me without
question from me that the minister had never raised the
issued. I despaired. Mr Clarke also had very strong views

about fur. In a country and a province where trapping played an important role, those were not very welcome.

The minister was not a guest of the Canadian Government, but we had managed to get him entry to the VIP lounge at the airport. When we got there, I asked for his ticket to give to the attendant who would check him in. When I looked at it I was surprised to see that it was going to take him much longer than usual to reach his next port of call, Seattle, just south of the US border in Washington State. He was routed in a very round about way. That coupled with the fact that I had learned that on his flight out he had not been booked in first class, suggested that perhaps some junior official in Whitehall was not over friendly towards him. You may not be surprised that when I took him towards the departure gate and was told I could go through security with him if I wished, I politely declined.

A welcome private visitor in our time in Vancouver was Carol Thatcher, an old friend of my wife's, whose mother was then Prime Minister of the UK. Carol was on a trip with other journalists looking at skiing in Canada. Early in the visit in eastern Canada she had broken her leg. In Vancouver she asked to stay with us and duly did so.

When the time came for her to re-join her colleagues to return to the UK we took her to the airport. It was a weekend and we were all very casually dressed. Checking in, an astute agent noticed that the name on Carol's ticket did not match the one on her passport. He queried it. Carol, leaning closer to him explained that for security reasons she travelled under the name of Fletcher, coincidentally the maiden name of my mother. She added that she travelled that way because her mother was the British Prime Minister. The agent looked disbelievingly at her, at which point I said that I could vouch for that. Looking pointedly at my casual attire, he asked, "And who might you be?" When I said that I was the British Consul-General he looked even more disbelieving. I had fortuitously put my tax ID card in my pocket and produced it. The change in his demeanour was startling. Despite his offers, Carol resolutely refused to be upgraded and insisted that she wanted to travel with the rest of her group.

The British Consul-General in Vancouver in my day was seen by many as a kind of supernumerary Queen's representative. It seemed to me that I was often asked to do things or attend events when the Lieutenant Governor was not available. Usually, that did not present a problem provided everyone understood, and we made sure that they did, that I represented the British Government not the Queen. There was, however one invitation which took me aback. British Columbia had a Youth Parliament. It met in the Chamber of the Legislative Assembly in Victoria, had a wooden mace and all the trappings of the real institution. I was asked by the organisers to play the part of the Lieutenant Governor and open the session. It seemed to me that for me, representative of the former colonial power, to ape the Royal deputy was not a good idea. I did not think that Federal Ottawa would think kindly of it nor would the High Commissioner. I declined. Everyone seemed very surprised. No-one seemed to see the point of why I had refused not even the Lieutenant Governor's Private Secretary who had been consulted. The High Commissioner, when I told him, was as horrified as I had been and entirely endorsed my line. Perhaps we were over sensitive, but I think not. I do not believe federal Ottawa would have taken it as lightly as the organisers in BC.

Vancouver for the bringing up of a young family was ideal. There was so much for Caroline to do. Victoria with its tourist attractions and museums was a firm favourite with her. Vancouver itself with its parks, planetarium and social activities also greatly appealed. Skiing was an attraction. At three, realising her chums at pre-school all skied, Caroline demanded, "Get me on skis Mummy". Grouse Mountain, thirty five minutes away and visible from the house, had a great class for little ones called Ski Wee. Caroline took to it easily and later as a seventeen-year old qualified as a Canadian ski instructor. Being so small, I suggested that someone would need not only to go with Caroline but to ski as well. Neither my wife nor I did so. So I said firmly that she being the younger was elected and must learn. She was game and undertook to do so. Grouse Mountain had a scheme to teach adults to ski. They undertook to do so in as many lessons as it took, usually six, for a fixed sum. Determined although she was, they lost money on my wife.

It was from Vancouver that we went on leave which took us around the world through Hawaii, Hong Kong, Thailand and the United States. It was a marvellous experience not least for our daughter who fell in love with the pink catamaran run by the hotel at which we stayed on the island of Oahu. Long afterwards, she would tell me that the pink catamaran was calling her back! Alas we never made it back.

It was during our time in Vancouver that Libby flew home to find and buy us our first house. She found a charming cottage at Eglwysbach in the Conwy Valley called "Tandderwen". We all loved it. Caroline during our leaves went to the local Welsh medium primary school adding Welsh to her French! Although it was also in Vancouver that she told me once that she was not Welsh. She told me that she had been born in Big Ben (the old Westminster Hospital in Horseferry Road). Somewhat facetiously I retorted, "Caroline if a cat has kittens in a fish shop it does not make them kippers". The look she gave me was something to behold.

One of the big events in the social life of Vancouver was the annual Consular Ball held at the Hotel Vancouver. It was usually attended by the Lieutenant Governor and other distinguished British Columbians. Although the corps in my day was half career and half honorary, it had to be chaired by a Career Officer in order to obtain duty free supplies. For two years I was the Chairman. The balls were always great fun. The Dean in my time was the Australian Consul-General, David Coombe, who had been Secretary of the Australian Labour Party. He was a political appointee. I was to meet him again later in London where he represented an Australian wine company.

One lovely person we got to know well in Vancouver was the late Mrs Olga Bell, Grannie Bell as we all called her. Then nearing ninety she was a most delightful person and a link with diplomatic history. Her late husband had served as our Consul General at Cologne during the later 1930s. He is to be seen alongside Neville Chamberlain in photographs taken when he visited Hitler in the run up to the Second World War.

One organisation of which, in 1987, I was proud to become a member was the Vancouver Round Table. Not to be confused with the Rotary organisation of that name, it is a select group which meets weekly to discuss local, national and international issues. Founded in the 1920s by academics and prominent business men, its membership is limited. My American colleague, Sam Fromowitz, was admitted about the same time as I was. I liked to think that we helped to open it to ladies who had previously been barred. They became eligible to join following a vote early in our membership. The first woman member was The Right Honourable Beverley McLachlin, now Chief Justice of Canada.

Another great Vancouver institution, which I admire, did not come into being until the year after I left the city.

That is, the Bard on the Beach, a Shakespearean summer festival, founded by the Bristol Old Vic trained Christopher Gaze. Libby and I joined after we began to holiday in Vancouver following my retirement.

Christmases in Vancouver were very much as they were in the UK. We had some lovely Christmas Eve dinners with local friends, especially Jimmy and Micheline Gill, Berwyn and Joan Roberts, and Evelyne Cazagnan. Jimmy, of Scottish parentage and french upbringing had had a difficult and distinguished war in the UK clandestine service. Berwyn was an old friend of my father-in-law from North Wales. An ordained minister, he too had had a hard war, as a Padre and prisoner of war in the Far East. Both, alas, are now dead. We much enjoyed their company and miss them. One Christmas we even played sardines in the lovely, rambling house of our friends, the Byrds, in West Vancouver. We were so lucky to have had such a great posting.

Despite our love for Vancouver, which we renewed when I retired from the FCO, after we had done the Board of Trade dinner for the fourth time I thought it time I moved on. So it seemed did the FCO. In April 1990 I was moved directly from Vancouver to be High Commissioner in Swaziland.

··· CHAPTER 14 ···

SWAZILAND

Our daughter, who, having attended French pre-school and having arrived in Vancouver barely able to speak at all, regarded herself as a little Canadian. She was not amused to learn we were going to live in Africa. Libby demanded to know how many cases of toilet paper we should take and what other supplies, until I told her that in many respects Swaziland was a first world country and that she need not concern herself about such matters. To test my theory, we made a trip to a large supermarket in Mbabane shortly after our arrival. We decided to see if we could find the unlikeliest items. We selected low-salt salt and sour cream. Not only did we find both, but also more varieties of Twinings tea than I had ever seen anywhere.

We travelled from Vancouver via London, Athens, whence Jim Smyth had been transferred, Cairo and with a transit stopover in Nairobi to Johannesburg. There we transferred to a Swazi Airlines plane for Matsapa Airport in Swaziland. Our trip was not without incident. The Olympic Airways pilot on the leg from Athens to Cairo had Caroline on his lap as we landed at Cairo. Fortunately, the co-pilot was flying the plane. It was banked to enable Caroline to see the hotel where we would be staying. We visited the Acropolis in Athens and the pyramids in Cairo. Caroline all of four years and eleven months was early introduced to history and archaeology.

With my agreement, the Deputy High Commissioner had gone on a brief local leave which had been planned. So when we reached Swaziland, we were greeted by the Second Secretary (Aid), later tragically injured so badly by car thieves in Nairobi that he died from those injuries.

For the first couple of weeks before I could present my credentials, I busied myself unofficially meeting people and learning of the work of the High Commission. The High Commission was housed in a purpose-built building erected at independence in 1968. It was a low high-rise with the ground floor let commercially. The UK staff consisted of a DHC, Second Secretary (Aid), Second Secretary (Admin and Consular), my PA and two Communicators. The non-resident DA was based in Maputo. In addition to the Commission staff I had under my wing the British Council representative, two UK-paid police officers, a three man British Army Training Team, an ODA-funded Chief Justice and a similarly funded tutor to the King. In addition to the UK-based there were a number of local staff at the High Commission including two drivers.

The residence had also been built in 1968 on land given by the late King Sobhuza. It was a rather ugly building of glass and concrete with metal handrails to the staircase. There were two downstairs loos in one of which was the urinal, which my wife insisted on having removed. We were very fortunate that we obtained funds to partly refurnish and to affect some internal improvements to the house. The drawing room and dining room had no separating walls or doors and presented the appearance of a long railway carriage. The improvements which were made included putting up separating walls and doors for the reception rooms, converting the dressing room upstairs to a private sitting room, changing light fittings and providing the fire place with a mantelpiece and improving the appearance of the staircase and the front entrance doors. The five bedrooms upstairs were closed off with metal "Rape Gates".

The staff consisted of a gardener and two indoor female staff one of whom was a cook. There was one vacancy. I was able to fill that with a man. John Mtembo had been a High Commission driver until he retired and before that had served as a steward at Government House during the colonial days. He actually hailed from Malawi, but had lived since long before independence in Swaziland. He was not always the sharpest or most efficient of men, but he was smart and his lovely smile was always a welcome to visitors. He continues to receive a pension paid personally by us.

It was John who was nearly responsible for a diplomatic embarrassment. At one formal dinner party which we gave, one of our guests arrived with two wives. Our dining table only seated eighteen and we were now nineteen. I told John that he would need to lay another place. Fortunately, I checked the dining room before we took our guests into dinner. For in the dining room as well as the main table was a small one intended for our use at breakfast. We never did; preferring instead to eat breakfast in the much cosier kitchen. John had laid the extra place on that small table. He had done so beautifully, complete with its own candles and flowers! He and I hurriedly dismantled his masterpiece and with some deft moving of things on the main table made room for the unexpected guest at the main table.

The number of missions at the time was small. When I arrived, Taiwan, whose Ambassador was Doyen, South Korea, the US, Israel and Mozambique were the only countries with resident Embassies. South Africa had a Trade Commissioner, the EEC a delegate and UNICEF and UNDP were also represented. A number of countries had honorary consuls. It did not take me long to undertake my necessary calls on the Heads of Missions.

After about two weeks the time for credentials arrived. They were timed for the evening. A rather ramshackle car was provided by the Ministry of Foreign Affairs to take us to the Palace in the valley, some miles from Mbabane, the capital. When I arrived I was asked to wait and did so with the Chief of Protocol and the Foreign Minister, Sir George Mamba GCVO who had been Swazi High Commissioner in London for many years and Doyen of the Corps. He told me that things were not done quite as they were at Buckingham Palace! After about an hour I was introduced into the King's presence. He was surrounded by a large crowd of men some in suits others in local dress. There were lights and TV cameras. I was in uniform and accompanied by my wife and the Deputy High Commissioner in morning dress. I presented my credentials and the Queen's greetings. The King said a few words in reply. After I presented my wife and the DHC the King invited me to sit beside him and conscious of the television cameras, we chatted about nothing very much for a while and the ceremony was over. We returned to the residence where the UK staff were gathered and enjoyed a glass of champagne.

I was now officially High Commissioner in Swaziland and began my task in earnest. The only instructions I had were to try if I could to persuade the King down the road to a more democratic form of government.

When I arrived in Swaziland, the King, Mswati III was twenty three. He had succeeded his father the remarkable King Sobhuza at the age of thirteen. He had been sent to school at Sherborne with the intention that he should then enter Sandhurst. Unfortunately, royal and political intrigue led to the deposing of the Queen Regent and to unsettled conditions. To end that situation the young King was brought back prematurely, crowned and charged with governing his small country.

Swaziland is almost exactly the same size as Wales with a population less than half of it. It is rich in resources, bauxite, coal, citrus, wood and cotton. It had achieved independence of the UK in 1968, the year the young King was born. The independence constitution had later been suspended, political parties banned and power concentrated in the King and the traditional councils of the nation. Over time some elements of the suspended constitution were reinstated. When I arrived, therefore, there were two governments. A bicameral Parliament, largely elected, with a Prime Minister appointed by the King and a Cabinet supported by a UK-style civil service. There were also a greater and smaller Council of traditional elders centred around the King's palace and with the Queen Mother as co-equal head of the nation. The system produced tensions. Tensions which one of my predecessors described as being between the young men in trousers up the hill (in Mbabane) and the old men in skins down the hill (at Lozita). Political parties remained banned although they not only existed, everyone knew their leaders and some of their views and doings were reported in the relatively free press. The European-style courts under a British-funded Chief Justice functioned. The Appeal Court was found by a number of senior South African judges who visited from time to time.

Against that background, I prepared for my first Queen's Birthday Party in June. It was an important occasion where the High Commissioner was expected to speak and through one of his brothers, the King would reply. The event was broadcast and televised. I decided to draw parallels with the UK, stressing that both countries were monarchies and gently urging the development of the constitutional form. We enjoyed a great advantage in that the King's English Language Private Secretary (nominally his tutor) was a British-funded former Gurkha officer, Major

George Lys. He drafted the King's reply. It was moderate in tone and contained some encouraging notes.

We were between American Ambassadors and the lady Chargé d'Affaires said to me after my speech that my line was a good one and that we should stand together and push in the same direction. That seemed sensible. Two weeks later I was present at the 4th of July Party in the American Residence Garden. The Chargé began her speech with the words, "We are met today to celebrate a revolution." Given that that revolution was against their King, it was an unfortunate choice of words. Speaking to me later, George Lys told me that when he had seen the advance copy of the American speech the King had been furious. George had written and torn up numerous draft replies. In the event the final version was dignified but cool. Shortly afterwards the new Ambassador, Steve Rogers, a Career Officer arrived. We became good friends. He decided that I should take the lead in the task both our governments had laid on us to persuade the King to modernise and he would offer support. Much later, poor Steve was often in the spotlight, on occasion accused of intervening in Swazi internal affairs when what he did was nothing compared with my activities.

Those were cloaked in secrecy and many including senior figures in the media took conscious decisions to keep them so having concluded that what I did was for the benefit of their country. Of course, long afterwards it became known that I had operated on behalf of the King in some negotiating.

I began a series of private audiences with the King, almost all of them arranged through George Lys, bypassing the Ministry of Foreign Affairs except when I had some formal communication from London to convey. I tried to keep the Prime Minister, Obed Dlamini, a democrat, in the picture.

The tone for my discussions with the King was set at
my very first audience by the King himself. President De
Klerk of South Africa had just taken the decision to release
Mr Nelson Mandela from detention. That threw Southern
Africa into some turmoil. Much as they abhorred apartheid
and the regime it supported, they had lived with it across
their borders and knew how to deal with it. Now they were
less certain and fearful of what would develop next door.
His Majesty referring to changes in South Africa asked me
what he should do. I replied formally that I could not
possibly tell him what to do, I was a foreign diplomat. For
the second time in my career I got the response, "No you're
not, you're the British High Commissioner."

Apart from political repercussions, Swaziland was concerned on economic grounds. They had benefited from
South Africa's international isolation. There was major
foreign investment in light industry in Swaziland out of all
proportion to its size and population. The products could
be sold in South Africa and the black African states would
buy them too. So, Cadbury Schweppes, Coca Cola, Pilkington Glass and others had put their plants in Swaziland
rather than in South Africa. On a visit to Pilkington's factory, I expressed some surprise that so much safety glass
was produced there for little Swaziland. The Managing Director put it in perspective by saying, "High Commissioner,
the amount of safety glass Swaziland needs we can produce
in an afternoon, our product is for export."

In 1991, the Commonwealth Heads of Government meeting was held in Harare. The King attended. He had learned
that our Ambassador in South Africa might have played a
role in facilitating contacts between the African National
Congress and the Government. When he returned to Swaziland, he told me that he had spoken both to the Queen
and to the Prime Minister John (now Sir John) Major and
asked if I could help him similarly. He reported that they

had been encouraging and told him to use me as he thought fit. He, therefore, wished me to talk to the leaders of the main underground political parties and see if some dialogue could be started. So began the strangest episode of my career. Shortly afterwards he asked me to work with one of his brothers, Prince Phinda, and a respected former diplomat and politician, the late Arthur Khoza. We called ourselves the Three Musketeers.

We held countless meetings with the young would-be politicians. Eventually we reported our conclusions to the King. He set up a commission which toured the country seeking the views of the people on the way forward. It was a long drawn out affair. The grumbles at the lack of progress grew loud. I became particularly concerned when at a party I gave for recently returned Sandhurst cadets and ones who had attended the Royal Military Academy earlier I was told by the young officers, with surprising candour, that I really must impress on the King the seriousness of the position.

I decided that I must do so. I asked to see the King but suggested that the Prime Minister be present. The three of us met and without compromising my young Army contacts I told the King that the process needed greater urgency. After almost two hours of discussion, I suggested that perhaps he should hear the Prime Minister's views, only for Obed to say, "It's not in our tradition." Fortunately, the King told him to speak up. At that point I suggested that I should leave so that they could continue in confidence and in their own language. When I saw the Prime Minister the next day, he thanked me for having him present the previous evening saying, "You see High Commissioner I can't talk to him about politics." I was astonished and thought that if the Prime Minister could not talk political matters with the King, who could.

After that there was more progress. The King asked the Three Musketeers, a name which caused him some amusement, to have further talks and advise him of the way forward in the light of the fall-out from the work of the first commission, known as Vusela I. We did so and in due course again reported to the King. We had agreed on names to put to him for him to consider appointing to a commission which would actually agree the principles of a new constitution. I left the King's presence when we reached the point where names would be mentioned, believing it right that he should hear them from his own people. There were senior councillors milling around near the Audience Room. I heard later that after my two colleagues had finished, the King left speedily ignoring the crowd and disappeared from the palace to a small house some miles away.

The next day, he announced the names for Vusela II. Although there were a few traditionalists among them, most were modernisers. They included the Chairman of the Human Rights Association and the Organising Secretary of the main underground party. Unfortunately, despite great efforts by the Prime Minister and by me, the latter declined to serve. His party was still highly suspicious of the King's motives.

In due course, Vusela II reported a very progressive set of principles which would have led to a democratic system and a largely constitutional monarchy with a few powers reserved to the King. A few weeks before I left Swaziland, the King received the report in the Royal Cattle Byre, the traditional site for momentous events. I was present, seated like everyone else, on the ground amid the cow pats. The King accepted the report in full and undertook to implement it. Alas, that did not happen. A new constitution did emerge after I had left, but it fell far short of what he had promised. Such are the fruits or lack of them of diplomacy.

Lest it be thought that my rather Vice-Regal role met with universal approval, I should record one difficult, though ultimately amusing event. The King's birthday had been celebrated in the usual way, but as I learned later, there had been a meeting dominated by traditionalists at which discussion had centred on making the American Ambassador and me persona non grata. It had been prompted by the fact that Steve Rogers had received the leading members of the underground party. That had been reported in the press as being "behind closed doors". I had done the same thing a little later. They had asked to meet me and I had agreed. Nothing subversive transpired at my meeting. Despite their political differences, Swazis were united in loyalty to their King who was their paramount chief. They were after all, almost unique in African in all being of one tribe. I doubt anything subversive occurred at Steve's meeting either. The traditionalists, however, were incensed.

I learned of the threat at the Israeli National Day Party. I tackled the Prime Minister about it who told me to stay calm. In fact wiser heads prevailed and as I learned later from someone who had been present, the Foreign Minister and others had said that they could not PNG us without severe repercussions. I was eventually summoned to the Ministry of Foreign Affairs and presented with a Note which complained but fell far short of what had been mooted. After discussions with London, a reply drafted in sorrow rather than anger was returned.

The amusement arose about ten days later. I had an audience with the King. He was due to make a private visit to London but we had managed to dress it up a bit. He was to be received by the Queen, and undertake a few other official engagements. The King asked me how arrangements for the visit were going. I replied that until about ten days earlier everything was going very well. He expressed surprise and asked what the problem was. I said that his government proposed to PNG me. He was astonished and said, "They weren't supposed to do that to you, only the American!"

One most pleasant event I was involved in was at the King's birthday parade in 1993. He had been made a Knight of the Venerable Order of St John. I asked if I could present it to him at the palace. He said no and that I was to be the guest of honour at the parade and do it publicly. I protested that he could not possibly have the representative of the former colonial power as guest of honour at his Birthday Parade. He overruled me and insisted. On the appointed day, I duly spoke to the assembled crowds in English with a Siswati interpreter. However, I decided to do the final paragraph in Siswati myself. I had been coached in it by one of my local staff and followed my wife's advice about delivery. She had noted that the cadences and intonations of Siswati bore some resemblance to the pattern which a slightly inebriated Italian might use speaking English. When I began in Siswati, a great roar of applause went up around the sports stadium. In his reply, the King ever gracious, said my Siswati was impeccable and put others who had lived in Swaziland for years to shame. Thereafter wherever I went I was greeted effusively in Siswati in a mistaken belief that I was fluent in it. I was not. Beyond a few greetings I was totally lacking in the language. What I had not realised was that my speech at the birthday parade had been broadcast nation-wide.

Another satisfying event was the dedication of the National War Memorial. At independence in 1968, the Commonwealth War Graves Commission had given money for one. It had been forgotten and become lost in the Swazi government accounts. After much research, it was located. A memorial was eventually erected on the site of what was to become the new Army headquarters. I dedicated it on Remembrance Day 1992.

Swaziland was not all intrigue and politics, although those often seemed byzantine. After all, we had a small daughter and she needed Daddy's time too. She was five when we arrived and eight when we left. She was fortunate in that Swaziland had a first class multi-racial primary school headed by a redoubtable Scottish lady, Mrs Mary Fraser. Some years later when we had to transfer our daughter from her original prep school which was closing its boarding house we learnt how good Sifundzani School was. The Head Teacher of our daughter's new school after she had taken their entrance test asked if we realised how knowledgeable and clever she was. In turn we reported that to the school she was leaving and thanked the Head for giving her such a good grounding. The Head said in response, "Don't thank me it is down to her early education in Swaziland."

Sifundzani was not the only good school in Swaziland. There was also a United World College, Waterford, providing multi-racial secondary education and a very fine technical school. That was set up and headed by an Anglican nun, Sister Judith Ellen Dean, a great lady whom both Libby and I much admire.

On one occasion, I became a small but vital cog in some behind the scenes international negotiations. The Dean of the Corps, the Mozambiquan Ambassador, wished to entertain the Corps. Curiously, or so it seemed to me, he was to do it in the capital of his own country, Maputo. The American Ambassador was on leave. I was rather unwell with some strange flu-like illness and felt unable to go. I came under great pressure to attend. Eventually, my doctor pumped me full of pills and still not one hundred per cent we flew to Maputo for a lavish dinner. It was only later that I learned that my presence was a necessity since without me the dinner could not have gone ahead. Only the United Kingdom and the United States of the embassies recognised both Mozambique and Israel. The Mozambiquans wanted private talks with my Israeli colleague with a view to opening diplomatic relations. I was the unwitting cover!

Maputo then was run down with many signs of the earlier civil war. It was, however beginning to repair and renew itself. We were to visit Maputo once more. In my final weeks, my European colleagues, all of whom although accredited to Swaziland were resident in Maputo wished to give me a farewell dinner. That time we drove. There were still many signs of the war along the way but Maputo itself was much improved.

I did make one other brief incursion into Mozambique, one which nearly caused an international incident. Early in my tour I received a briefing by the British Army Training Team and the Swazi Army and police about border security. The Swazis suggested that we should visit the border and the Mozambiquan customs post with whose occupants they had good relations. We did so. However, across from the customs post was a small Army post. Whether it was the uniform worn by the BATT Commander or our presence as a whole, I do not know, but they became a bit agitated and ordered us at gun point into their hut while they went off to seek a superior. After a few minutes, I realised they had effectively left us unguarded. So I wandered out to light my pipe, the BATT Commander joined me. Casually and still fussing with my pipe he and I sauntered towards the border gate some yards away. We passed through without incident and that was that. Our Swazi friends were still on the Mozambiquan side, but I never heard of any repercussions.

One of my functions was supervision of our aid programme. We had a number of very good projects, but the one which brought us the most publicity and the most gratitude was the Heads of Missions' Small Projects Fund and Small Gifts Scheme. Those funds amounting to about thirty five thousand pounds which I could use at my discretion. Every time I did presentations, mostly from the Small Gift Scheme, it was the lead item on the national television news. One of the things I used it for was to help Women's Groups. We discovered a supply of treadle Singer sewing machines which I bought up. I gave the machines to a number of groups.

Another fine project I was able to help from those funds was the Swaziland Hospice At Home. It was set up to bring palliative care to cancer sufferers and Aids victims in their own homes, in line with local tradition. Founded by a Macmillan-trained nurse who was the wife of one of my police advisers, Stephanie Wyre, it operated initially from an old caravan which I funded. Later with lottery funding it was able to build a clinic. Libby served as its Chairman. When the Wyres who hailed from Gwent, as I did, returned to the United Kingdom they set up a Friends of Swazi Hospice. They kindly asked me to be its Patron as I still am. The ODA as well as funding projects supported a number of experts, two police advisers, the fire service chief, George Lys and the Chief Justice. The latter caused me some problems. When the one I had found there on arrival left to take a post in Namibia, we had to find a new one. It was not easy. Eventually, a New Zealander serving as a puisne judge in Bermuda agreed to serve. He had a good report from the Chief Justice of Bermuda whom I knew well. Unfortunately, he did not get on well with the officials of the Ministry of Justice. I seemed to spend a lot of time trying to pour oil on troubled waters. After my departure, I learned that things got worse and eventually he left. The ODA did not fund another and Swaziland turned to South Africa, which had the same legal system, Roman Dutch law, to provide the Chief Justice.

Being big fish in a small pond, we felt the need for frequent breaks from our goldfish bowl existence. Fortunately, we had friends next door in South Africa. Pretoria and Johannesburg were only three or four hours' drive away. In Pretoria was an old friend who had been my First Secretary (Economic) in Pakistan, Paul Haggie, his wife and their two small children who were about the same age as our daughter. In Johannesburg as Consul-General was John Doble who had been Consul-General Edmonton when I was in Vancouver. They provided us with much needed R & R for which we remain very grateful.

The Haggies were responsible for our acquiring a pet. They had a Golden Labrador bitch. When she had pups, our daughter was desperate to have one. She won the tussle of course. So entered our lives, another Tanya. She was for the rest of our time in Swaziland to provide us all with many happy hours. When we left we found her a good home in Mbabane with the sister of a friend we had in Vancouver, the broadcaster Dave Abbott. It really is a small world. That was not the only Canadian connection with Swaziland. We were visited there by Bill Armstrong, a former President of the Vancouver Club and his wife, Barbara, whose son, Christopher, was teaching at a school in the country for which I provided assistance from my Small Projects Fund.

Despite its small size and relative distance from the United Kingdom we had visitors. Apart from official ones from the FCO and Mozambique, we had visits from friends. One such was from Richard Luce and his wife, Rose. He had visited Swaziland once before as a Minister in the FCO. I was able to take Richard to see the King. Tanya was to be the cause of a big upset with Richard. We had a swimming pool in the garden which Caroline and her friends loved. One day during the Luce visit, they were swimming, Tanya on guard at the side. My wife and the Luces were sunning themselves beside the pool. Libby was summoned to the house for a telephone call. When she returned there seemed to be mayhem. It transpired that Richard had decided to join the girls in the pool. Tanya, no doubt believing he was a threat to Caroline, jumped in and went for him. Richard has a very weak back and Tanya pushing him was too much for it. She had also scratched him. Thoughts of rabies and suggestions of putting down drew anguished cries. Fortunately, Tanya was not rabid and eventually peace was restored.

Another private visitor was Sir David Gibbons and his wife, Lully. David had been a very successful Premier and Finance Minister of Bermuda. The day they arrived, the King decided he wanted to come to supper and to talk with me, Prince Phinda and Arthur Khoza. My wife took the Gibbons to dine in one of the big hotels. The King arrived at 7pm. Arthur joined us but for some reason Prince Phinda never turned up. I discovered later that he had sat outside the gates waiting to be summoned by the King. When David Gibbons returned to the house, he joined us in the dining room and encouraged the King to follow Bermuda's example as an offshore banking and re-insurance centre for Southern Africa. He offered model legislation and some expert advice. The King was appreciative and suggested he meet the Prime Minister. That he did but nothing ever materialised.

The King did not drink very much and throughout dinner had only imbibed apple juice. After dinner when John brought in the liqueurs, he spotted a square bottle and asked to try it. It was an unopened bottle of Cointreau. I opened it and passed him a liqueur glassful, pushing the bottle to his side of the table. The King left just before 3am.

When I checked the bottle, it was only half full! Some weeks later when I saw the King he asked what the liqueur was and described it as beautiful. But he went on to say that he could remember nothing of the day following the dinner and very little of the one after that!

One high-level visitor who came after the Harare Conference was Sir Lyndon Pindling, the Prime Minister of the Bahamas. He was well received even if his name was variously spelled as Pinkling and Pindley. The King gave a state banquet for him and the second night the Prime Minister gave a large dinner. The latter was somewhat chaotic. I was asked to sit on the top table. When I asked why, I was told I was the senior High Commissioner to which I replied, "I'm the only High Commissioner". For whatever reason, the head table was taken in first. We were followed by a milling throng. The Chief of Protocol becoming increasingly agitated told the security personnel that they must not sit at the tables. He asked the diplomats to sit at tables one side of the head table and Ministers on the other. It was well nigh impossible for them to comply. Finally in desperation he said, "You can see I'm harassed, sit where you like."

Apart from our friends the Luces, the late Dame Marjorie Bean and David and Lully Gibbons from Bermuda, the only other significant visitor we had in our time in Swaziland was (now Dame) Veronica Sutherland, then Deputy Chief Clerk. She paid us a pastoral visit. She was later our Ambassador at Dublin.

There were of course very many big Royal events at which the Diplomatic Corps was usually expected to be present. They could be tedious. Tradition dictated the King should keep people waiting. He often did. The worst of such occasions happened when the Queen Mother was to undergo a ceremony to ensure that her marriage to the late King was wholly lawful. Rather late it was discovered that some part of the complicated ritual for the marriage had been omitted. It was felt necessary to undertake it to avoid any doubts about the King's legitimacy and his right to the throne. The Corps were bidden for 9.30am. By 1pm with no sign of the ceremony getting underway, the entire Corps decided it had had enough and left. It was the only occasion in my career when the whole diplomatic community rebelled to a man. We later received an official apology through our Mozambiquan Dean.

The other occasion which stands out was when the King visited a British commercial enterprise. My wife and I were the only diplomatic couple present. After the ceremony there was to be lunch. My wife was asked to have lunch with the King's wives. I and the other men with the King. As we entered the hotel Libby saw the lunch buffet with its smoked salmon, asparagus and other goodies. However, when she was in the room where she and the wives were to lunch she discovered to her horror that the King had provided for his wives a great local delicacy - a cow's stomach. Her appetite rapidly disappeared.

One of the saddest events in our time was the death of a young British couple. They had a young son, Merigan. The husband, Brian, had been at University College Bangor and considered himself an honorary Welshman. He worked for a forestry company. The couple went up in a light plane with the fire spotter on the last trip of the season. Tragically, the plane crashed and they were killed. I was asked to give the eulogy at the funerals. Because I was due to see the King, and local culture would have prevented me doing so if I had been recently close to a death, I could not do so. I wrote it and my wife bravely delivered it for me.

One of the great events of the year was the annual Reed Dance. At this, young woman presented to the Queen Mother reeds which they had collected for re-thatching her

Kraal. They also danced. They did so bare-breasted and traditionally the King used the opportunity to choose a new wife. One year my parents-in-law were visiting. They with us were seated in the Royal Box. They were seated next to the Prime Minister's wife who was a bit embarrassed. My mother-in-law said to her how wonderful it all was and how much my father-in-law had been looking forward to it. In her typical way she said to him, "You have been looking forward to it haven't you?" He replied dryly, "Yes, I like reeds."

One hilarious event was our attempt to sell a British plane to Swazi Airlines. The company brought a plane to demonstrate. The King decided to take the trial flight. He was, as always, accompanied by a large entourage. They all piled aboard the aircraft. There were so many that every seat was occupied and they were strap hanging in the aisle. Wisely, they were forced to disembark before the pilot took off.

As in Sierra Leone so long ago, so in Swaziland I was to become aware of a dark side to the country. Witchcraft still flourished, despite the country's adherence to Christianity. Here it took the form of Muti. It was not confined to Swaziland, but had adherents in South Africa too. Muti is particularly horrible and involves the use of parts of small children, especially those of powerful men. The belief is that consuming such will give power to the user. The only time I was really frightened in Swaziland was the day when I was giving a stag lunch. Our nanny in a somewhat agitated manner reported that she had not found Caroline at Sifundzani at the end of school. Caroline, as the daughter of the British High Commissioner, was perceived as being powerful and would have been a prime candidate for Muti particularly as elections were pending. We feared she had been taken. With much frantic searching Caroline was finally found, totally unconcerned and oblivious to our anguish, at the school swimming pool.

One event we attended which had amusing repercussions was a royal wedding of one of the King's innumerable sisters. There was dancing in which I joined rather energetically. Writing later to congratulate me on my CMG, my colleague, our ambassador in South Africa (now Sir) Anthony Reeve had added that he did not think that a man nearing sixty could be such an enthusiastic dancer. Unbeknown to me, South African television had carried some film of the wedding and of the antics of the British High Commissioner. Some months later at another function as the Queen Mother shook my hand, she said, with a smile, that there would alas be no dancing at that event.

In May 1993, a few weeks before I was due to retire, I received a telegram from London informing me that in the Birthday Honours Her Majesty proposed to make me a Companion of the Order of St Michael and St George (CMG). I was honoured, but surprised. My career had hardly been meteoric and I had not expected to receive it. A few weeks later the local chapter of the Order of St John advised that I was to be appointed an Officer of that Venerable Order. Not one, but two awards all in the space of a few weeks.

In the last twelve months that I was in Swaziland, we were visited by the late Mark Patey, then Chief Immigration Adjudicator of the UK. He had served in the Colonial Service in Swaziland and was visiting friends. We had met him some years earlier when he visited Pakistan. On that occasion we had entertained him and his colleague to dinner. As it happened, my wife conscious of my approaching retirement had applied for an appointment as a fee-paid Immigration Adjudicator. Although a qualified Barrister

she did not wish to return to the Bar. However, she realised that with a daughter to educate my pension would
need supplementing. Given her pending application I did
not think it right to entertain Mark on this occasion. In the
event she was appointed and for our last year in Swaziland
flew to the United Kingdom for three weeks at a time to
carry out her duties. She usually contrived that they should
coincide with Caroline's half terms. On a brief leave in the
UK we had dinner with the Pateys. Mark asked me what
I intended to do in retirement. He had discovered that I
was an admitted solicitor and suggested that I might join
my wife as a fee-paid Adjudicator. That, after an interview
and a three month sanitising period, is what I did.

That was not our original intention. Towards the end
of my time in Swaziland we applied for and were granted
landed immigrant status for Canada. However, that was
only valid for six months. In our usual way we failed to get
organised in time and never made it to Canada. We did,
however, buy a home there, in Vancouver.

I reached sixty on 26th July 1993. I had used up all
my leave before that. So on the morning of my sixtieth
birthday accompanied by Libby and Caroline and escorted
in another car by my deputy, now technically Acting High
Commissioner, I was driven in the Daimler with flag still
flying to the South African border. After hand shakes, we
changed vehicles and I was driven across the border into
South Africa and into retirement from the Queen's service.
So ended almost forty years of service to the Crown in one
capacity or another.

We were to return to Swaziland for the 25th Anniversary celebrations which occurred about six weeks after my
retirement. We flew on an HS125 of the Queen's Flight.
Prince Edward (now Earl of Wessex) was to join the flight
at Harare and represent Her Majesty at the celebrations. It

was a long flight involving constant refuelling stops including at Jeddah and at Harare in Zimbabwe where we were able to meet again with Richard Dales, the High Commissioner and his wife Elizabeth, who had been with us at a conference in Zambia and Bob Dewar, who had been Desk Officer for Pakistan when we served there and who had been the first visitor my wife had at the Westminster Hospital after giving birth to Caroline. It was great fun to see both of them again.

One rather amusing if embarrassing event was when I changed my clothes just before we were due to land at one of our way points. Suddenly, the plane lurched and I ended up, in the royal cabin, with my trousers around my ankles and the royal cipher on the back of the seat above my head. Fortunately, my wife had no camera.

About a year or so after my retirement I became Chairman of the Swaziland Society and served in that capacity for several years. Amongst those I welcomed to its gatherings over the years were the King, the Prime Minister and many other distinguished Swazis I had known and worked with during my time in Mbabane.

··· CHAPTER 15 ···

RETIREMENT

In fact my departure from Swaziland wasn't quite the end of my Crown service. Because of my Immigration Adjudicator (later Judge) appointment, I was to continue to serve the Crown in a wholly different, this time judicial capacity, for the next fourteen years.

Mark Patey died three months after I started work as an adjudicator. Thereafter, I served with three Chief Adjudicators, Judges David Pearl and Hubert Dunn and the late and greatly missed Sir Henry Hodge, a judge of the High Court to whom my wife was deputy.

In 1997 Judge David Pearl, Mark Patey's successor as Chief Adjudicator, suggested that with the increased number of Adjudicators then nearing two hundred, a professional association should be formed. A small steering committee of which I was a member was formed. It put together a draft constitution and arranged an inaugural general meeting at Kings College, London. Following that meeting I was elected the first President of the Council of Immigration Judges and undertook, subject to re-election to serve for three years to get the organisation off the ground.

I decided to follow lines I had learned in the Diplomatic Service and began a round of calls on people whose support we needed. Foremost among them was Sir Tom Legge, Permanent Secretary to the Lord Chancellor and

Lord Woolf, then Master of the Rolls and Head of Civil Justice. Both were enormously welcoming and encouraging. Another official I believed important to us was Michael Huebner, then Chief Executive of the Court Service. He later moved across Victoria Street to become the Deputy Secretary in the Lord Chancellor's Department. Over the years I found him greatly helpful and we became and still are firm friends both of us now retired. Officials in the Lord Chancellor's Department especially the Head of Judicial Department II directly concerned with our Tribunal also proved helpful. During my Presidency, they were successively Edward Adams, John Tanner and Mrs Christine Pulford. Although, we did not always agree and I did not always succeed in persuading them to my point of view, they invariably tried to meet the concerns of my members. We usually discussed those over a beer in "The Albert". Although we had to have formal meetings I found the former style most useful.

When I assumed office I made a list of what I would like to achieve. When I left office three years later, to my intense satisfaction, I found that all but one, the title Immigration Judge, had been achieved. That latter was to be conferred some years later. In my three years' service I had two Deputy Presidents. Firstly Catriona Jarvis and for the second and third years Michael Rapinet who was a Vice-President of the Immigration Appeal Tribunal. He was to succeed me as President at the Annual General Meeting in Oxford in 2000. At that meeting, my colleagues conferred on me the title, President Emeritus. It sits lightly. The only duties appear to be to propose the loyal toast at the Annual Dinner and a vote of thanks to the President at the Annual General Meeting.

I think that the achievement which most endeared me to my colleagues was persuading HM Inland Revenue that we should enjoy a tax allowance similar to that afforded to other judicial officers.

An amusing incident which pointed up the change in my role occurred shortly after I retired from the Diplomatic Service. We were at a reception at St James' Palace for the Pilgrims (the Anglo-American Society). Her Majesty The Queen was to attend. Before she arrived, an usher spotting the crossed UK/Swazi flag badge in my buttonhole suggested I should be presented. In due course I was. I was introduced as lately High Commissioner in Swaziland but now retired. The Queen asked what I was then doing. I said that she had kindly taken me back on the payroll and that I was an Immigration Adjudicator. Her Majesty's response suggested to me that perhaps she envisaged me stamping passports at Heathrow.

Of the many thousands of cases I heard in my fourteen years as a judicial officer, I remember only two. Very early on I was faced with a case involving the rather arcane subject of domicile linked with polygamous marriage. I knew nothing of either issue. It took me ten hours to research and write the judgement! My new role was a steep learning curve.

The other was shortly after the coming into force of the Human Rights Act 1998. In a case before me it was pleaded that to return an appellant to Russia would expose him to the degrading conditions which then existed in that country's prisons. I recall writing in my judgement refusing the appeal that, "It cannot have been the intention of Parliament to make the British taxpayer responsible for the prison conditions in every country on earth". Astonishingly, it was never appealed.

In retirement we returned to Wales. We thought that our cottage in North Wales was both a bit small and rather far from London where my wife and probably I were going to have to earn some money. We, therefore, bought a house in Chepstow in the county where I was born and raised. The added attraction was that it was only thirty miles from my wife's parents who had moved from Chester to Cardiff.

The county of my birth, Monmouthshire, was one of the thirteen Welsh counties created by the Act of Union of 1536 in the reign of the Welsh Tudor King, Henry VIII. Before that, it did not exist. That Act also replaced Welsh law with English civil law and introduced to Wales the Office of Sheriff. For some time some people were confused about the status of Monmouthshire. It arose primarily because when subjected to English law Monmouthshire was made part of the Oxford circuit rather than the Wales and Chester circuit. That, however, no more made it an English county than Chester's attachment to the Wales circuit made it a Welsh city. My Monmouthshire is now called Gwent and has been since the local government reforms of the Heath government. It comprises the 1536 created geographical county plus the town of Caerphilly and its hinterland which were taken from the neighbouring county of Glamorgan.

Monmouthshire was part of the Diocese of Llandaff and when the church in Wales was disestablished under the 1914 Act, the churches in Monmouth were disestablished, save for two on the Herefordshire border. Those border parishes were allowed to choose. Two of them opted to be part of the Diocese of Hereford and of the Church of England.

One year, not knowing quite what to give my daughter Caroline for Christmas, I decided to try to trace a family tree. Working then at Taylor House in Rosebery Avenue in London which shared a building with the Family Record Office, I set about the task in my spare time. The later years on both sides of my family and my wife's were easy. I had been helped on my mother's side by a second cousin who had traced the Fletcher line to my great-great grandfather born in Gloucestershire in 1791. On Libby's side I had both her parents to consult. Even so some interesting facts emerged. The dates of the tombstones of Libby's maternal great-grandparents at Seven Sisters in Glamorgan did not tally with dates and ages given elsewhere. Libby's great-grandmother was the daughter of a farmer on whose farm her great-grandfather worked as a jobbing carpenter. They married at Neath Registry Office, unusual for church and chapel-going folks in Wales in those days. Of course, in those days marriage without parental consent under the age of twenty one was not allowed. I suspect, although I never had proof, that they eloped since her great-grandmother could not have been twenty one although she said that she was! On my mother's side, I discovered that my grandfather had been born in Pembrokeshire one month after his parents had married!

On Libby's side too we had a strange experience. Libby's maternal grandmother had married a congregational minister who died tragically young. He was the son of a Breconshire farmer and grew up at Glynllech Farm. We travelled one day to find his father's grave. It was in a non-conformist chapel cemetery. It was a very distinctive memorial being of pink granite with a pitched roof-type top. A year or so later and after her mother had died, we were invited by friends in Essex to spend the weekend. They suggested that we visit an interesting church nearby. Walking through the graveyard we saw down a slope a pink granite tomb with a pitched roof top. Intrigued we took a closer look. Astonishingly, it recorded that it was the burial place of a woman whose maiden name was Price, that of Libby's mother. It went on to record that she was of Glynllech Farm Breconshire and Greenstead House Essex. Who was she? Clearly she was of Libby's family. Alas with my mother-in-law and her sister now dead there was no-one to ask. Perhaps one day we will try to connect the dots and find out how she came to end her days so far from her native Wales.

On my father's side, with help, the line was easier to trace for longer. We have even attended divine service in the ancient church of Llanbrynmair where so many of my ancestors were baptised and married. We also much later visited Alveston from whence hailed my mother's paternal line. In the church we met the archivist. When I said that my mother's maiden name was Fletcher, he pointed to the many memorials all it seemed to me dedicated to Fletchers and said that even today almost everyone in the village is called Fletcher. Tracing that line may not be so easy.

Apart from my work as an Adjudicator I felt the need to help especially in Wales. I had on retirement, become the representative of the Swazi Ex-Service Organisation on the council of the British (now Royal) Commonwealth Ex-Services League. That had been suggested to me by Brigadier Mike Doyle then the General Secretary of the League who had been our Defence Adviser when we were in Pakistan. However, with my O St J, I thought I should do something for that organisation. I offered my services and became a member of the St John Council for Gwent. A few years later when Welsh local government was again reorganised and the Gwent St John Council was replaced by a St John Council in each of the five unitary authorities which replaced the administrative county of Gwent, I became Chairman of the St John Council for Monmouthshire and a member of the Chapter of the Order in Wales. Those jobs gave me much satisfaction and I thoroughly enjoyed the six years I held them.

I had had a relatively fulfilling life due in large part to the largesse of the rate payers of my home town in providing me with a great education. It seemed to me that I should try to repay that in some way. Not long after I retired, I was asked to go and see Paddy (now Lord) Ashdown at the House of Commons. I did so. He suggested to me that I should consider standing in the European Parliament Election as a Liberal Democrat candidate in North Wales. With my eurosceptic views and less than fluent Welsh, I did not think that I could realistically do so. Had I accepted his invitation I would, of course, have returned to my political roots. Had I been elected I might well have had a lucrative retirement or even ended up in the Westminster Parliament. In the event, I declined the offer and heard no more of a political career. I also thought that I was too old to enter local politics, but when I was asked if I would be interested in serving as High Sheriff of Gwent, my wife and I agreed that although it might prove expensive, I should. It would provide an opportunity to do something for Newport and the county of my birth. As my wife put it, "It was pay back time".

Her Majesty duly pricked my name and on 4th April 2004, I made the prescribed declaration in the old Number 1 Crown Court, now the Coroner's Court Room, in Newport's Civic Centre. I knew that building well. As a boy at the High School I had attended quarterly meetings of the Borough Council as their guest. I had determined that although in Gwent Shrieval declarations and the activities of High Sheriffs were often low-key, mine would be rather more high profile. It seemed to me that such an ancient office with its potential for good should be visible. The old Court Room was full not only of civic leaders from all over Gwent, but with relatives and friends both old and new from far and wide. I was particularly pleased that three men who in 1944 had joined me at the High School were there, one, John Harris, as my Chaplain. That six friends from Canada, including Dick Vogel in Canadian naval uniform, should also have made the effort to attend was a very special pleasure to me. I had the great honour of making my declaration not before the usual Justice of the Peace but before the then Senior Presiding Judge of England and

Wales, Lord Justice Thomas, a distant cousin of my wife. Because of my RAF service, the central band of the Royal Air Force agreed to provide a brass ensemble to play incidental music and the two National Anthems at the end of the ceremony. A splendid contribution to the day they made.

We followed the declaration with a Sheriff's Breakfast for the Circuit Judges and others who had attended in robes and our friends who had come to support me. On the next day, Sunday, I had my Shrieval service in St Mary's Priory and Parish Church in Chepstow, which is a lovely, partly Norman foundation. The Bishop of Monmouth preached the sermon. The station band of RAF St Athan accompanied the hymns led by the Chepstow Choral Society. I read the second lesson. The first was read by my eighteen-year old daughter. She had on a lovely Eau de Nil outfit with matching hat. Unfortunately, the wind had caught it as she arrived at the church. She hadn't been able to re-fix it securely. Throughout her reading it seemed that it might slide off her head at any moment. I am sure that the attention of most of the congregation was on that rather than on the words she read, albeit she read them beautifully and that she seemed oblivious to the impending descent of the hat. She was in her first year at Oxford and a number of her friends from Worcester College had come to be in the congregation to afford her moral support.

It is little understood that High Sheriffs are unpaid and do not even receive any expenses. Moreover, in most counties there is no administrative support, save that afforded by the Under Sheriff. I was fortunate. Newport City Council (it had become a city in 2002) provided a room for me next to the Mayor's Parlour. They also, on repayment, afforded me the services of a part-time Secretary, the ever helpful Vanessa Duggan.

In June, the Civic Heads of the five Unitary Authorities changed. The new ones were to serve with me until I left office in April 2005. All were drawn from the Labour Party which then controlled four of the five authorities. Monmouthshire County Council had changed hands at the May 2004 election and was then controlled by the Conservatives but the new Chairman, Mrs Olive Evans, a Labour councillor who had been Vice-Chairman was nevertheless installed. My own home town of Newport had a long tradition of choosing as Mayor the senior councillor who had not passed the Chair regardless of party affiliation or which party controlled the council. I had always been proud of that and often quoted it in my years overseas as an example of British politics at its best.

The tradition went back to the late 1920s when a heavily Conservative council which had always chosen the senior councillor as Mayor found that that role had reached a Labour man, Alderman Frank Quick. To their credit he was made Mayor and a good one he proved to be. When in 1945 the political complexion of Newport changed the controlling Labour Party continued the fine tradition. Newport's Mayor for 2004/5 was Paul Cockeram. He and his wife Vicki, gave the city great service and became our good friends. The same was true of their counterparts in the other four authorities in Gwent. We still spend a weekend together every year.

The High Sheriff has the opportunity to travel all over the county of Gwent. Over the centuries, his official functions have been whittled away. Originally the only representative of the Crown in each county with very wide powers, by 2004 it was second in the county to the Lord Lieutenant and largely confined to a ceremonial role. Having originally been responsible for law and order, most High Sheriffs involve themselves in charitable work connected to that area. In Gwent, a former High Sheriff, Ian Donald, had set up a

charity, with the rather unwieldy name: Gwent Shrievalty
Police Trust (GSPT). It provided funds to projects designed
to keep young people off drugs and away from crime. It was
chaired by the Chief Constable. The High Sheriff, his predecessor and the High Sheriff in nomination were members
as were other worthies and such former High Sheriffs as
cared to continue to serve. I remained a member until the
Trust was dissolved and its role incorporated in a wider organisation. Much of my time as High Sheriff was taken up
with trying to raise funds for the GSPT by such devices as
a ball and concerts.

One other good cause I tried to help was the restoration
of the Newbridge Memorial Hall. I had known that building
as a boy when my aunt often took me to the cinema it
housed on Saturday evenings. It had fallen into disrepair
and a local committee was making great efforts to raise
funds to restore it. I was able to organise a concert in the
village of Abercarn next door to Newbridge, with the aid
of a ladies choir of which I was patron and the school choir
from my old primary school, Gwyddon. We succeeded in
raising some hundreds of pounds. Not a lot, but every little
helped.

I had two main charities as High Sheriff, the Gwent
Shrievalty Police Trust and the Royal Air Force Association. To raise funds for the latter I was able to arrange a
concert by the band of the RAF Regiment.

Altogether during my year I undertook around two hundred and fifty engagements. I bought a second-hand Jaguar
car and found a most excellent driver. Together, and often
with my full-time employed wife at weekends, we travelled
thousands of miles from Caerphilly in the west to Chepstow and Monmouth in the east and from Newport in the

south to Brynmawr in the north and most places in between. Wherever we went we were most warmly welcomed. I suspect that some did not often see the High Sheriff.

One lovely event we attended was the candlelight Carol Service held by Barnardo's of which Libby was a national Trustee in the largely roofless Tintern Abbey on the banks of the Wye. I read one of the lessons.

Two other events which I was particularly happy to host at the Civic Centre were for old friends and former colleagues. The former was a lunch for as many Old Boys of my year at Newport High School as were able to attend together with the President and Secretary of the Old Boys' Association. The other took the form of a lunch reception at the Civic Centre followed by a visit to the Roman fort and amphitheatre at Caerleon within the Newport city boundaries for members of the Foreign and Commonwealth Office Association. Both were highly enjoyable and I was very grateful to the catering staff at the Civic Centre and the General Manager at the Newport Transport Undertaking for all their help.

What struck me very strongly was how many people in so many places gave sterling service to their communities entirely voluntarily, and for the most part wholly unremarked. There are High Sheriff's awards for community service. They had not been made in Gwent for three or four years. I resolved to use them. I made seven spread over all five authorities. We made an event of the presentation of them accompanying it with a champagne reception in Newport Civic Centre. The five Civic Heads attended as did the South Wales Argus photographer. I found the local press very helpful. I had met the Editor of our leading paper, the South Wales Argus, right at the beginning of my year. He was the first person I entertained to a drink in my room at the Civic Centre.

What struck me about the awards, however was that all the recipients were women and of a certain age. I asked if there was anything for secondary school age people. There was not. I decided to create a High Sheriff's award for citizenship in secondary schools. The High Sheriff's Association printed certificates for me and I bought and had inscribed five "silver" cups one for each authority. With the help of the Chief Education Officers of the five authorities I selected five awardees. I presented the certificates and cups to each, usually at school assembly.

Our youth was frequently the subject of a bad press. That was something I was certain needed to be redressed. The Editor of the South Wales Argus seemed to agree with me, at least they covered every award ceremony.

I had chosen as my theme for the year, Youth. It was, therefore, great that I was able to support a wonderful organisation called Gwent Music. When the Gwent County Council disappeared, the new authorities agreed to contribute to Gwent Music thus enabling it to survive. It organised training and concerts for young musicians throughout Gwent and supported an orchestra and brass band. I was amazed at how many young people gave up so much of their free time in the evenings and at weekends to dedicate themselves to music. They, and countless others in youth organisations all over the county gave the lie to the bad press which our young people so often received. I was pleased that I was also able to give a cup to Gwent Music for them to award for musical achievement.

The one regret I had in my year was that despite the best efforts of others in the local authorities, I was not able to hold, as I had planned, a one day conference of young people and county authorities. That would have explored the needs and aspirations of youth and enabled the five authorities, all of whom shared similar problems, to share their experiences.

My old school, Newport High School on Queen's Hill, had gone. It had been replaced by a new High School at Bettws on the outskirts of the city. The pupils wore the same colours as I had done and it possessed the old honours boards and the assembly hall platform furniture with which I was familiar from my days as a prefect. I decided to visit it again and to donate a cup which they decided to award for achievement. The first award was made to a girl, not thought to be academically front-rank, but who had nevertheless got herself to university and was to become a lawyer. They kindly invited me to be the guest speaker at Speech Day and to present the prizes. I also visited my old primary schools in Newport and Abercarn, the latter now a Welsh Medium School. I went to both in black court dress complete with fore and aft cocked hat and sword. The first question I was asked in both was, "Are you a pirate mister?" and the second, always from a young lad was, "Is that sword real?"

Wishing to meet as many of my fellow citizens of the county as possible, I decided one way was to attend divine services at churches throughout the five authorities. I had, of course, to attend the civic services which each Civic Head held, but with the help of my Chaplain I was able to attend others all over the county. Perhaps, however, the most significant church service of my year was the one held in St Woolos Cathedral in Newport. It was traditional for the presiding judges of the circuit to hold two services each year in Wales, one in the north and one in the south. The latter alternated between Llandaff Cathedral in Cardiff and St Mary's Church in Swansea. During my year, and in recognition of Newport's newly acquired city status, they decided to hold the South Wales service in that city. It was the first time since the ending of assizes, thirty years earlier, that St Woolos had played host to the Legal Service.

Although much of the responsibility for it fell on the Circuit Administrator and his staff, I was heavily involved. We received every assistance from the Dean (Very Reverend Richard Fenwick) and the Minor Canon (the Reverend Mark Soady) now both our good friends. I also had great help from the Gwent police. The Chief Constable (Mike Tonge) not only provided motor cycle outriders as the judges preceded by my car drove from the Mansion House to the Cathedral, he also agreed to provide six stalwarts in helmets and white gloves to carry the halberds used in the 19th century by the High Sheriff's pike men. They lined the lychgate entrance to the Cathedral. The Royal Regiment of Wales also turned up trumps providing trumpeters to sound two awe-inspiring fanfares as the processions entered and to introduce the National Anthem at the end of the service.

The day of the service was bright and sunny. It was a most splendid occasion. The legal procession with its bewigged barristers, recorders and circuit judges, the five Civic Heads, my fellow Sheriffs from the other Welsh counties in court dress and their Lord Lieutenants in uniform made a colourful picture. We had an additional splash of colour in the person of Lancaster Herald, a friend of a former Sheriff, in his scarlet uniform. He headed the Gwent procession. On this occasion our Lord Lieutenant (Simon Boyle) yielded precedence to me. I brought up the rear preceded by my cadet from the St John Ambulance Brigade carrying my sword ahead of the two presiding High Court Judges in their scarlet robes and Lord Justice Thomas in his black and gold state robe.

I was charged with reading the first lesson in Welsh and English. I was relieved that my often inadequate Welsh not only got me through the former but earned me praise from the wife of the Junior Presider, herself a fluent Welsh speaker.

After the service I gave a reception at the Civic Centre followed by a luncheon for the senior judges and others. As we sat down to lunch it started to rain, but it did not affect a memorable day.

St Woolos Cathedral stands at the top of Stow Hill in Newport. The site has been occupied by a Christian house of worship for over twelve hundred years. It was chosen as pro-Cathedral when the Diocese of Monmouth was carved out of Llandaff after the disestablishment of the Anglican Church in Wales. Much of it is old, some of it Norman. It is in need of urgent repairs. An Appeal Committee of which I am a member is urgently trying to raise the three million pounds it now needs for repairs.

One of the remaining functions of the High Sheriff is to attend upon and protect Her Majesty's High Court Judges, although the real protection, fortunately, is afforded by the Gwent police. During my year no red judge sat in Newport. However, I sat with the Recorder of Cardiff, John (now the Honourable Mr Justice) Griffith-Williams during a rather gruesome murder trial. I also sat with the senior local Circuit Judge (HHJ David Morris) in another case. In both cases, providing lunch for them and Counsel on both sides. The circuit judges very kindly gave a lunch for my wife and me just before I left office.

The senior judges attending the Legal Service had robed at the Mansion House courtesy of the Mayor. We were to receive much hospitality in that lovely house, as well as at the Civic Centre in Newport both during my year, and later from that year's Deputy Mayor, Alan Morris and his wife Jane, when he became Mayor a few years later. The other Civic Heads also extended warm hospitality to us at their civic dinners or lunches and on numerous other occasions. We were very grateful to them for that and for their support to us in so many ways during my year of office.

I also had enormous support throughout my year from the redoubtable Harry Pollaway, Civic Toastmaster of Newport. Then nearing ninety he officiated at my Declaration and at numerous other functions throughout my year. He was, in his ninety fourth year, again to come to our aid and add his colourful and ever humorous personality to our daughter's wedding.

There is one official function retained by High Sheriffs. They are the Returning Officers for the parliamentary constituencies in their counties. In practice, of course, the electoral arrangements are made by the Registration Officer, usually the local authority Chief Executive. Nevertheless, if he so chooses, the High Sheriff can read the results. Greatly to my disappointment, the General Election of 2005 took place six weeks after my term of office ended.

My last engagement before I left office was to entertain the five Civic Heads, the Chief Constable, the Under Sheriff and my Chaplain to a farewell dinner. We held it in the Chairman's Suite at the Monmouthshire County Hall in Cwmbran. It was a jolly evening and my friends were kind enough to make some very agreeable comments about us both and about our service to Gwent.

As the Foreword notes, our daughter married on 31st January 2009. She became Mrs Christopher McCabe, wife of a DPhil student of Physics at Worcester College whom she met as an under-graduate. She remains in Oxford as a trainee accountant with Grant Thornton. On 7th March 2009 we watched proudly as both of them graduated in the Sheldonian Theatre, she as a Master of Mathematics and Philosophy and he as a Master of Physics.

I continue to enjoy my retirement filling it with my charity work and learning Italian and Dutch. The latter inspired by our friends in Flemish-speaking Bruges which we visit regularly.

CHAPTER 16

ROYAL COMMONWEALTH
EX-SERVICES LEAGUE

Apart from the shrieval year and my paid employment as a fee-paid judge for fourteen years, I busied myself with charity work. I have written of the GSPT and the Order of St John. The other charity in which I have invested time in retirement is the Royal Commonwealth Ex-Services League (RCEL). I began as Swaziland's representative, but in 2002 was asked to represent the Royal Canadian Legion as its ex-officio member of the Executive Committee (Board of Trustees) as well as the Commonwealth Council. With my Canadian associations I was delighted to do so. That meant that I worked closely with the Dominion Secretary of the Royal Canadian Legion, Brigadier General Duane Daly. Our Canadian associations were strengthened when in 1997 we bought an apartment in Vancouver. We used it a great deal, every school holiday, whilst our daughter was at school. Apart from my duties as Canadian Trustee, I had already taken on others when I succeeded the late Sir Philip Bridges QC as Honorary Legal Adviser. Although not onerous, the latter role enabled me to work closely with successive Deputy Grand Presidents (Chairmen), two distinguished retired 4-star Generals, Sir Ted Burgess and Sir Sam Cowan and with three Secretaries General (Sam Pope, Brian Nicholson and now Paul Davis).

One of the nicest men with whom I served on the RCEL Executive was the late Lord (Jack) Wetherall, former Speaker of the House of Commons. He was charming and a great help to us all with his wide knowledge. When ill-health led to him standing down it was a great loss. The other peer who served with him on the Executive, and still does, is Viscount (John) Slim. His association through his late father Field Marshal Slim with Burma and Burma Star veterans and his own service with the SAS amongst other units was and is invaluable as is his link with Australia whose Trustee he is.

The other task which fell to me as Legal Adviser was to chair the Steering Committee for the Triennial Conferences of the League. Those conferences, in Cape Town, Barbados, London, Ottawa and Accra were great occasions to meet veterans from all over the Commonwealth. They included some who had served in the Second World War. The first event at every conference was the service at the local war memorial. Each of the conferences, save for Ottawa, was attended for at least part of the time by His Royal Highness the Duke of Edinburgh, Grand President of the League for many years. He takes a very close interest in its affairs. It was at the Barbados conference that I was, as Honorary Legal Adviser, charged with presenting a paper on the future of the league with which Prince Philip did not wholly agree. I dreaded the task. In the event, His Royal Highness was very gracious and we were able to secure the agreement of conference to it without incurring Royal displeasure.

Over the years I have had to make very many speeches. I have always been grateful for the grounding in public speaking which I received at my old school and the honing it received later at the LSE Students' Union and the Oxford Union Society. Of all the ones I have made I think that one of the better ones was that made to close the Ottawa

Conference of RCEL in June 2005. A short extract from the end of it appears at Appendix B.

The League with its fifty six affiliated organisations in forty eight countries dispenses funds to help impoverished veterans, especially of the Second World War, in Commonwealth countries. All who served the undivided crown and are in need are eligible. In the Caribbean, the charitable work is undertaken for the League by the Royal Canadian Legion using funds it gathers itself. As the years pass, the number of crown veterans is expected to fall markedly. The League is now, therefore, concerned to establish how to retain the links when its purely charitable function comes to an end. In 1921 when it was set up it had no charitable function. It may be that we shall find the future model in its origins. In any event, a study group on which sit representatives of the founder members (England and Wales, Scotland, Canada, Australia, New Zealand and South Africa) is presently considering the future with a view to reporting to the next conference in Malta scheduled for 2012.

It has been a fascinating life, although as someone once said, it was rather a roundabout route from Newport's Corporation Road Elementary School to the office of the High Sheriff of the county in Newport's Civic Centre.

APPENDICES

FAMILY TREE

WATKIN Morris Thomas   married   18 April 1664 Mary
(of Llanerfyl)

John WATKINS   married   Catherine
b. 29 Jan 1668 Llanerfyl

Hugh WATKINS   married   Priscilla Fletcher
b. 1702 Llanerfyl   b. 16 July 1710 Carno
    d. 11 March 1766 Carno

Thomas WATKINS   married   1. 10 Feb 1766 Elizabeth Miles
b. 3 May 1741 Carno   2. 5 May 1772 Jane Humphries
    b. 22 April 1745

David WATKINS   married   12 May 1798 Mary Owens
b. 20 May 1775   b. 1770
d. 29 Mar 1849 Llanbrynmair   d. 28 October 1844

John WATKINS   married   1 May 1830 Elizabeth Jones
b. 25 December 1803   b. 1805 Carno
d. 1851   d. 1885

Evan WATKINS   married   21 Aug 1859 Emma Broadbent
b. 1830 Montgomeryshire   b. 1833
d. 17 November 1906   d. 5 September 1903

George WATKINS   married   25 Dec 1890 Ann Maria Moore
b. 27 Mar 1871 Wolverhampton   b. 5 September 1871
d. 24 June 1938 Newport, Mon.   d. 28 Dec 1932, Newport, Mon

James Edward WATKINS   married   7 April 1928 Gladys Ann Fletcher
b. 4 Mar 1905 Newport, Mon.   b. 15 January 1896 Newport, Mon.
d. 29 Dec 1981 Newport, Mon.   d. 25 January 1942

Brian WATKINS   married   1. 26 October 1957 Thelma Waite
b. 26 July 1933 Newport, Mon.   b. 2 October 1935
    Mark Gareth Watkins
    b. 18 November 1958
    2. 31 Dec 1982 Elisabeth Arfon-Jones
    b. 2 July 1950
    Caroline Ann Arfon Watkins
    b. 31 May 1985

EXTRACT FROM THE CLOSING ADDRESS TO THE 29TH CONFERENCE OF THE ROYAL COMMONWEALTH EX-SERVICES LEAGUE, OTTAWA, 23RD JUNE 2005

"I know that it is our tradition, but it is especially fitting in this the year which marks the 60th anniversary of the ending of the Second World War through which I lived, that we should have begun our Conference at the National War Memorial to honour the memory of those did not live through it. The memorial across the road is dedicated to the fallen of this great land of Canada. On Sunday it was the focus for the very many hundreds of thousands of the Commonwealth and Empire who in two world wars went forth from every corner of the globe and did not return. They came from great cities and sleepy villages, from market towns and busy seaside ports. From the frozen wastes and rolling prairies of Canada, from the sun-baked plains of India, the high Savanna and dark green jungles of Africa and Malaya. From tiny dots in the great Pacific and in the warm Caribbean sea. From the sheep farms and cattle ranches of Australasia and from the lovely hills and vales of my own land. Why?

If we could ask them, their replies would be couched in modest words. Some might even have some difficulty in answering why. But the truth is that they shared a common devotion, a common devotion to concepts and values which some, too many, today view with amusement or even disdain. They, however, the dead and those who survived, believed in ideals which need majestic words to convey - duty, honour, sacrifice, loyalty, patriotism.

As we begin the long journeys to our homes across the seas, may we resolve that in the years to the next conference we concern ourselves not solely with the raising of funds for the welfare of those who survived, not solely even with the great task of caring for those in other lands unable now to care for themselves, but to make our young and those who succeed them aware, not just on Armistice Day, that they are what they are because a great ideal which still survives was paid for at a very great price. For whatever our national political context, whatever our particular view of the past, there is one inescapable historical truth. There is no nation on this earth which would today be quite as it is had that price not been paid.

I believe that that message cannot be spoken too often or too loudly in our evermore uncertain and often very self-indulgent world. For me it is summed up in simple words, but ones which are perhaps the most poignant in the English language, carved on a memorial stone at Kohima in Burma, **"When you go home, tell them of us and say, for your tomorrow, we gave our today."** "